W9-BYA-512

MORE SMART CHOICES FOR PRETEEN KIDS

Group

Loveland, Colorado

MORE SMART CHOICES FOR PRETEEN KIDS

Copyright © 1999 Group Publishing, Inc.

All rights reserved. No part of this book may be reproduced in any manner whatsoever without prior written permission from the publisher, except where noted on handouts and in the case of brief quotations embodied in critical articles and reviews. For information, write Permissions, Group Publishing, Inc., Dept. PD, P.O. Box 481, Loveland, CO 80539.

Credits

Thanks to contributors John Cutshall, Mikal Keefer, Julie Meiklejohn, Pamela Shoup, and Michael D. Warden, and to all the authors who contributed great lessons to Active Bible Curriculum®.

Compilation Editor: Jim Hawley
Editor: Michael D. Warden
Creative Development Editor: Dave Thornton
Chief Creative Officer: Joani Schultz
Copy Editor: Bob Kretschman
Art Director: Jean Bruns
Cover Art Director: Jeff A. Storm
Computer Graphic Artist: Digitype
Cover Designer: Anita Cook
Illustrator: Gary Templin
Production Manager: Peggy Naylor

Unless otherwise noted, Scriptures taken from the HOLY BIBLE, NEW INTERNATIONAL VERSION®. Copyright © 1973, 1978, 1984 by International Bible Society. Used by permission of Zondervan Publishing House. All rights reserved.

Library of Congress Cataloging-in-Publication Data
More smart choices for preteen kids.
     p.   cm.
   ISBN 0-7644-2110-7 (alk. paper)
   1. Christian education of children. 2. Christian education—
   Activity programs. 3. Preteens—Religious life.   I. Group
   Publishing.
BV1475.2.M565 1999   98-33173
268'.432—dc21   CIP

10 9 8 7 6 5 4 3 2 1   08 07 06 05 04 03 02 01 00 99

Printed in the United States of America.

contents

INTRODUCTION

The preteen years are challenging...both for the kids and for you. Ten- to twelve-year-olds often receive mixed messages about whether they're still children or mature young people. Kids this age are starting to develop their independence, so they're questioning authority and tradition more than ever before. They're noticing that the world is full of unfamiliar and exciting possibilities. Add those developmental qualities to our fast-paced, grow-up-soon world, and the preteen years can become a turning point.

Will your kids get through them with a stronger, active faith?

You want your kids to *use* their faith in their new world. You want them to turn to the Bible and God for decision-making help. And you want them to react to their world with good, smart choices.

More Smart Choices for Preteen Kids picks up where *Smart Choices for Preteen Kids* (Group Publishing, Inc., 1998) left off. Just as in that popular resource, active-learning lessons can help your kids prepare for real-world choices. Because these lessons creatively explore issues kids struggle with, the activities will intrigue your kids. They'll be caught up in the learning.

Each lesson addresses an attainable goal that's based on Scripture, so the activities give your kids the solid biblical background they need to make choices. The lessons also encourage kids to do what God wants them to do. They'll walk away from these lessons with a greater understanding of the choices they face, of how their faith influences those choices, and of what God wants and why; they'll be armed with specific responses to those choices.

Because the preteen years can be a turning point, *More Smart Choices for Preteen Kids* strives to help you help your kids enter their teenage years with a stronger faith, a better understanding of Scripture, and a commitment to do what God wants them to do. With these active, pertinent, and biblically based lessons, your kids' faith can develop a "growth spurt" that will last the rest of their lives.

THE FALL

Kids face powerful temptations. Whether it's helping a friend cheat on a test or considering taking drugs, the number of temptations preteens face is alarming. To make things worse, the world often seems to suggest that resisting is too difficult and perhaps even unhealthy.

This lesson helps kids understand that they are not prisoners of temptation. Instead, it helps them see how they can rely on God's grace and strength to resist temptation when it comes.

Opening

TWENTY TEMPTATIONS

(For this activity, you'll need newsprint, markers, and a prize.)

Form teams of no more than four. Give teams each a sheet of newsprint and a marker. Have teams each designate a scribe who'll write on the newsprint. Say: **We all face many temptations every day. On "go," list twenty temptations you might face in a typical week. I'll give you the first one to list, but it'll be up to you to list the rest. The first team to list twenty must call out, "twenty temptations." Then the other teams must stop writing. Write so we can read your ideas. If an idea is illegible or isn't really a temptation, it won't be counted. Also, if you list the same or similar idea twice, it'll be counted only once.**

The team that lists twenty temptations first wins a prize. The first temptation is "cheating on a test." Ready? Go!

When a team calls out "twenty temptations," call time. Collect the newsprint sheet from that team, and go over the items listed. Ask the entire group whether to accept questionable items. Then count the number of items on each of the other teams' lists, and declare the winner. Give a prize (such as candy or snack food) to the winning team. Ask:

● **How did you feel during this game?**

● **Were you tempted to cheat? Explain.**

● **How is being tempted to cheat in this game like the temptations you just listed?**

Goal:

To help preteens recognize and resist temptation.

Scripture Verses:

**Genesis 3:1-24;
1 Corinthians 10:13;
Hebrews 2:18; 4:15**

Have kids vote on which temptation listed is most common and which is most rare. Then say: **Some of the temptations we face are small. And some are major, potentially life-changing temptations. But whatever their size, we all face temptations. Today we'll take a look at a familiar Bible story that can help us better understand temptation and how to resist it.**

Reflection and Application

Raid the Cave

(For this activity, you'll need masking tape and a knotted rag.)

You'll need a large room for this activity, or you may do it outside. Use masking tape to mark off a 10x10-foot area. This will be the "bear's cave."

Place a knotted rag—the treasure—in the center of the cave. Have a volunteer be the "bear" who'll guard the treasure. The rest of the students must try to swipe the treasure without being tagged by the bear. The bear may not pick up the treasure. People tagged inside the cave must freeze where they are. The person who gets the treasure becomes the next bear. If no one gets the treasure within two minutes, the bear wins and a new bear is picked.

Explain the game to the students. Then play for eight minutes. Kids will probably become frustrated if they can't get the treasure or if they can't guard it well. That's OK; you'll discuss their feelings after the game.

When time is up, regroup for a discussion. Ask:

● **How did you feel as you played this game? Explain.**

● **What risks did you take in this game?**

● **How are those risks like the risks we take when we give in to temptation?**

● **Did you choose to race right in or wait outside the cave for the right opportunity? Why or why not?**

● **Did you enjoy the risks in this game? Why or why not?**

● **How is the way you played this game like the way you face risks in everyday situations?**

Say: **Sometimes the risks associated with temptation seem minor. But when we give in to temptation, we're risking more than being tagged in a game.** Ask:

● **What are risks associated with temptations you face in real life?**

Say: **To better understand temptation, let's take a look at the familiar story of Adam and Eve.**

WHaT IF?

(For this activity, you'll need Bibles, paper, and pencils.)

Form groups of no more than five. Give each group a Bible, paper, and pencils.

Say: **Read aloud Genesis 3. Then talk about what might've happened if Adam and Eve hadn't given in to temptation.** Allow three minutes for groups to read and discuss the chapter in Genesis. Then have kids discuss these questions in their groups:

● **What made it difficult for Adam and Eve to resist the temptation to eat the fruit?**

● **How is this situation like the temptations you face?**

● **What's one temptation you have a hard time resisting? Explain.**

● **How might things be different if you never gave in to that temptation?**

Have groups read together Hebrews 2:18; 4:15; and 1 Corinthians 10:13. Then have them discuss these questions:

● **How can these verses help us overcome temptations we face?**

Form new groups of no more than three. Have group members quickly think of a tempting situation they might face. Then, one by one, have groups act out their situation up to the point where someone must decide whether to give in to the temptation. For example, a group might role play kids asking friends to go with them to a questionable movie.

When the skit has stopped, have other kids call out ways to avoid the temptation. For example, kids might say, "Say no and walk away" or "Tell your friends they shouldn't go."

After groups have presented their skits, reread 1 Corinthians 10:13 aloud. Say: **We learn from Genesis 3 that giving in to temptation can have disastrous results. But we learn from the New Testament that no temptation is too great to overcome. Still, it's not always easy to know the right thing to do in tempting situations. Let's take a few minutes to create a plan for dealing with temptations.**

Make a Commitment
....

PRESCRIPTioNS

(For this activity, you'll need tape, pens, and a copy of the "Prescriptions" handout [p. 9] for each person.)

Distribute a "Prescriptions" handout (p. 9) and a pen to each person.

Form pairs. Then say: **Jesus was tempted in every way that you and I are. Yet he didn't sin. He understands how difficult it is to resist temptation. He wants to encourage us to be strong and not to give in to temptation.**

In fact, God has made a way for us to escape every temptation that comes our way. With your partner, write a prescription for resisting temptation. Include practical ways to overcome temptation such as "avoid tempting situations" and "ask God to help you." Imagine that Jesus is writing this prescription to you and your friends. In a few minutes we'll read some of these prescriptions.

Allow four to six minutes for partners to complete their prescriptions. Be available to help kids during this time.

Then have kids each read their prescriptions to the class. After each prescription has been read, have kids say what they liked about it. For example, someone might say, "Your prescription is a good idea" or "Your prescription makes a lot of sense." Encourage kids to share only positive thoughts for each prescription read.

Have kids tape their handouts to the wall. Say: **Think about a temptation you're facing. Then come up to this wall and silently read the prescriptions. Choose one or more ideas from these prescriptions to use in the coming week as you face temptation.**

Keep the prescriptions on the wall for a few weeks to remind kids they can resist temptation.

Closing

TOUGHEST VICTORY

(For this activity, you'll need index cards and pens.)

Form groups of no more than five. Give kids each an index card and a pen. Say: **On your index card, write one of the toughest temptations you've been able to resist or overcome by God's grace. Don't put your name on the card. After you've finished, tear your card into as many pieces as there are people in your group. Give one scrap to each person in your circle.**

After kids have done this, say: **Carry these scraps in your wallet or pocket this week to remind you to pray for the people in your group. Ask God to make each of you strong enough to overcome whatever temptations come this week. The scraps will also remind you that others are praying for you.**

Form a large circle. Have kids each offer a one-sentence prayer asking God to help them resist temptation in the coming week.

PRESCRIPTIONS

Jesus was tempted in every way—just as we are—yet he didn't sin. Because Jesus was tempted, he's able to help those who are tempted. God is faithful; he won't let you be tempted beyond what you can handle.

Adapted from Hebrews 2:18; 4:15; and 1 Corinthians 10:13.

Imagine you're a spiritual doctor with a specialization in resisting temptation. In consultation with your partner, write a prescription for resisting temptation to be used by young people.

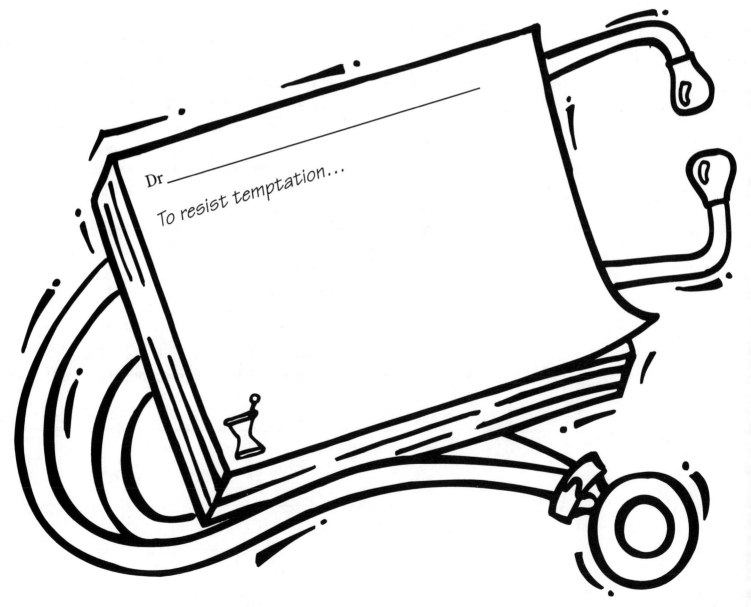

Dr _____

To resist temptation...

Permission to photocopy this handout from *More Smart Choices for Preteen Kids* granted for local church use.
Copyright © Group Publishing, Inc., P.O. Box 481, Loveland, CO 80539.

THE FLOOD

Goal:

To help preteens trust God to rescue them from difficult situations.

Scripture Verses:

Genesis 6:1–9:29; Hebrews 11:7

Young teenagers often feel like helpless captives of their circumstances. They can be paralyzed by their inability to be and do all they wish for themselves.

This lesson helps kids see that without God we are powerless. But by understanding and receiving the redemption Jesus Christ offers to all who trust him, they can be freed from powerlessness and live abundant lives.

Opening

TRUST SEARCH

Form groups of no more than six. Say: **Search this room for objects that remind you of specific occasions when you overcame a limitation by trusting a person or God. For example, you might take off your shoe and tell about a time someone went with you to do something scary or difficult for you to do, or you might pick up a pencil and tell about a time you made it through a pop quiz with God's help. The person whose first name's first initial is first in the alphabet will begin.**

After the first person finds an object and tells about it, have the next person in alphabetical order go on a similar search. Encourage kids to describe their objects and tell their stories quickly.

After everyone has found and described an object, call the kids together and form a circle.

Ask:

● **How did you feel as you described your trust experience?**

● **What did you learn from the stories your group members told?**

Say: **Today we're going to explore what it means to trust God. We'll begin by examining ways our faith can help us escape bad situations.**

Note

If you have more than ten students, have all the kids go on their search at the same time; then have kids take turns telling the meaning of the items they chose.

THE BEST WAY OUT

(For this activity, you'll need tape and "Good" and "Lousy" signs.)

Tape a "Good" sign to a wall at one end of the room and a "Lousy" sign at the other. Clear the furniture from the center of the room so students can move easily between the signs. Have kids stand facing you in the middle of the room.

Say: **Today we're exploring how God rescues people who trust him. To get a feeling for the escape routes we choose, I'm going to read possible ways out of situations you might face. If you think the escape plan described is a good one, walk to the end of the room with the "Good" sign. If you think it isn't a good plan, walk to the "Lousy" sign. If you aren't sure how you feel, stand somewhere in the middle.**

Read the "Escape Plans" in the margin one at a time. For each situation, allow time for kids to find their positions between the "Good" and "Lousy" signs. Then ask:

● **Why do you think this is or isn't a good way to get out of this problem?**

● **What alternate plans could you suggest?**

● **How do you think God might help someone out of a fix like this?**

Before you finish reading the last situation, stop the activity suddenly and say:

Something's wrong here. Hear that sound? Pause. **It seems our room is filling up with water. The doors are blocked and the windows locked shut. You have two minutes to decide how you'll respond to this situation. I'll keep you posted on how high the water is. Right now it's up to your ankles.**

Have kids band together to discuss how they'll try to escape the flood. If they come up with a plan they think will work, quickly give them a reason it won't work. For example, if kids say they can climb through the ceiling tiles to escape, tell them the tiles are blocked on the other side. Every fifteen seconds, update kids with the height of the water. After a minute, the water should be up to the shortest person's neck. Have kids work together to stay above the water as they talk about what they'll do. Be sure to play along, and keep your head above the waterline too.

After two minutes (or when the water level is about to cover someone's head), gather kids in a circle and pray, asking God to rescue them from this flood. Then say: **Wait...the water's stopped coming in. In fact it's subsiding.**

▶ ESCAPE PLANS

▶ 1. Your friends ask you to go to the mall the same day your mother wants you to help with a birthday party for your little sister. When they pressure you to come along, you tell them you have too much homework.

2. The lunchroom is noisier than usual. Every time the lunchroom monitor turns her back, a french fry flies. You know a food fight is about to start, so you say to your friends, "I think I'll go to the library to study for next week's math test."

3. While playing a pickup baseball game in the street, you hit a home run off your neighbor's car and put a dent in the hood. After you tag home, you keep running back to your house.

(Escape Plans, continued)

4. A fight breaks out in the aisle next to your table in the lunchroom at school. You jump between the two who are fighting to get them to stop slugging each other.

5. You're at a friend's house with several kids, studying for next week's English test. Your friend's parents aren't home. Your friend offers everyone a beer. You take the beer and pour it into a houseplant a little at a time so no one will notice you're not drinking it.

6. Your friends plan to go to a popular but violent horror movie, and they invite you to join them. You really don't enjoy all the "blood and guts" stuff and don't want to see the movie. You say, "I've heard that film was terrible. I don't want to see it."

Let kids know when the water is finally out of the room. Then form a circle. Hand out imaginary towels and ask:

● **How did it feel to try to get away from the flood by your own wits?**

● **How did it feel to give up trying to escape on your own and pray to God for help?**

● **How is this experience like times God helps you through difficult situations?**

● **What are some ways God rescues you from difficult situations?**

Say: **Our flood was nothing compared to the flood Noah endured. Let's see what we can learn from how Noah responded to his situation.**

The Bible Experience

Faith Charades

(For this activity, you'll need Bibles.)

Form groups of no more than three. Have groups each find a place in the room away from other groups. Give each group a Bible.

Have groups read aloud Hebrews 11:7, paying attention to what it says about Noah's faith. Then have groups search for evidence of Noah's faith in the account of the flood in Genesis 6:1–9:29.

Have groups each choose one evidence of Noah's faith to act out in a charade for the entire class to guess. Tell kids each charade is to be acted out without props or speaking.

Allow groups five minutes to decide what to act out. Then have groups perform their charades. After each charade, have the rest of the group guess what the charade portrayed. Then have the group members who performed the charade tell what they were presenting about Noah's faith. Ask:

● **What did you discover about Noah's faith?**

● **What can we learn about faith from this story?**

Say: **Trust is an important element of our relationship with others. Without trust, we can't develop a healthy relationship with people. It's the same way with God. We may not always get the response we want, but if we trust God he'll help us find an "escape plan" for difficult situations.**

FaitH SCULPtURES

(For this activity, you'll need Bibles and pipe cleaners.)

Form a circle. Give each person a pipe cleaner. Have a volunteer read aloud Genesis 9:12-16. Then say: **Think for a couple of minutes about your relationship with God. Has Jesus rescued you from difficult situations or problems in your life? Has he helped you when you have had trouble in your relationships at home or at school? Shape your pipe cleaner into a sculpture that illustrates one way God has helped you or rescued you from trouble.**

Allow two or three minutes for kids to create their sculptures. Then have kids each describe their sculptures. Ask:

● **How do you feel about your relationship with God?**
● **Why is it important to trust God?**
● **How can you begin to trust Jesus more this week?**

After several kids respond to the last question, ask kids to form pairs and pray for each other, asking God to help them trust him to rescue them whenever they have problems.

Closing

HOW'S YOUR TQ?

(For this activity, you'll need pens and a copy of the "How's Your TQ?" handout [p. 14] for each person.)

Give kids each a "How's Your TQ?" handout (p. 14) and a pen. Say: **These handouts won't be shared with anyone else, so don't be shy in filling them out. When you've completed the handout, take a couple of minutes to reflect on your score. Then think of ways you can be more thankful each day.**

Form a circle, and close by having kids thank God for rescuing them from difficult situations. Encourage kids to keep their handouts as reminders to be thankful for all God's done for them.

How's Your TQ?

You can trust God to rescue you from difficult situations. One way to show that trust is to thank God often for all he does for you—through his Spirit, through the Bible, and through people he has placed in your life. Use this handout as a gauge to measure how thankful you are for God's help in your life. Total your points at the end to measure your own "Thanks Quotient," or "TQ."

Fill in the blanks, and write your score in the column on the right.

1. Write the name of one friend you said "thank you" to this past week. _____
Give yourself 5 points for writing the name and 10 more points if you remember
what you said "thank you" for. _____ POINTS _____

2. Write the name of one family member you said "thank you" to this past week.
_____
Give yourself 5 points for writing the name and 10 more points if you remember
what you said "thank you" for. _____ POINTS _____

3. Give yourself 15 points if you wrote a thank you note to someone
this week. _____ POINTS _____

4. Think about your last birthday or Christmas (whichever is freshest in your memory),
and list the gifts you received.
_____
_____
_____
Give yourself 1 point for each gift you can remember saying "thank you" for and
5 extra points for each one you wrote a thank you note for. _____
_____ POINTS _____

5. In 30 seconds, list gifts God has given you. Give yourself 1 point for each thing
you've thanked God for this week.
_____
_____
_____ POINTS _____

6. When was the last time you thanked Jesus for dying to rescue you from sin?
_____
_____
_____
Give yourself 1 point if it's been more than a year, 5 points if it's been less than a
year but more than a month, 10 points for less than a month but more than a week,
15 points for less than a week, and 20 points if you did it today. You can still get
20 points by thanking him now, before you write the number. POINTS _____

Now total your points, and put your total "TQ" here. TOTAL ☐

Less than 30 points . . . . **Think of ways you can be more thankful.**
31 to 74 points . . . . **Keep on thanking!**
More than 75 points . . . . **Don't stop now! Spread the contagious thank you!**

Permission to photocopy this handout from *More Smart Choices for Preteen Kids* granted for local church use.
Copyright © Group Publishing, Inc., P.O. Box 481, Loveland, CO 80539.

WHAT HaPPens WHen YOU Die?

The greatest mystery of life is probably death. No one knows what it's like to die—but everyone dies. Kids today are intrigued by death, so they seek answers to a seemingly impossible question: What happens when you die? With the popularity of beliefs such as reincarnation, kids are getting mixed messages about what happens after they die.

This lesson encourages kids to look to the Bible to discover all they need to know about what happens after death.

Opening

Deadly Drawings

(For this activity, you'll need newsprint, tape, markers, the "Drawings" list in the margin, scrap paper, and chocolate candies.)

Tape a large sheet of newsprint to the wall, and set out markers. Give each person a piece of scrap paper. Say: **We're going to play a game of "Deadly Drawings." Each of you will silently draw a picture that describes a common phrase. You'll each have twenty seconds to draw your picture for others to guess. If no one guesses your phrase, you'll have to suffer the dreaded "crumpled paper" torture. That is, the other class members will crumple up their papers and toss them at you. If someone guesses your phrase, you and the guesser each will win a chocolate candy.**

Have the person with the shortest hair be first to create a drawing. Show the artist the first phrase in the "Drawings" list in the margin. Cover up the other words and phrases so he or she doesn't see them. Then give the artist twenty seconds to silently draw a picture of the phrase. If someone correctly guesses the phrase, give the artist and the guesser each a chocolate candy. If kids don't guess the phrase, have them toss crumpled papers at the artist.

Give each person an opportunity to draw a phrase from the list. If you have more than twelve kids, add your own phrases or words to the list.

Goal:

To help preteens understand the biblical promise of resurrection.

Scripture Verses:

Job 19:25-27;
John 11:25-26;
Romans 8:10-11;
2 Corinthians 5:1-9;
Ephesians 2:1-5;
1 John 3:1

▶ DRaWinGS

- dead duck
- dead in the water
- deadhead
- dead tired
- working myself to death
- death by chocolate
- die laughing
- die-hard
- deathbed
- death-defying
- dying to know
- wake the dead
- _____
- _____
- _____

Permission to photocopy this box from *More Smart Choices for Preteen Kids* granted for local church use. Copyright © Group Publishing, Inc., P.O. Box 481, Loveland, CO 80539.

When kids have each created a drawing, form a circle. Give chocolate candies to kids who didn't get them earlier. Then ask:

● **How did you feel as you created your drawing?**

● **How did you feel if you received the dreaded crumpled-paper torture?**

● **How is that like the way some people feel when they think about the subject of death?**

Say: **In this activity, you may have felt many different feelings, such as anger, guilt, or fear. Thinking about death brings about some of the same feelings. Many of those feelings come from not knowing what happens when someone dies. Today we're going to let the Bible help us learn what happens when we die.**

Reflection and Application

THiS iS YOUR LiFe, LiFe, LiFe...

(For this activity, you'll need white and black beads and a paper bag.)

Say: **Eventually, everyone dies. And because death is inevitable, people are curious about it. People wonder what happens after death. One common belief is that people are reincarnated, but the Bible doesn't teach us about reincarnation; it teaches us the truth—about resurrection. Though they may sound somewhat similar, reincarnation is very different from resurrection. Let's find out what reincarnation is.**

Tell students to each imagine that instead of being given one life to live, they have to live as many lives as it takes to become perfect. Put some beads in a paper bag, one-fourth white beads and three-fourths black beads. (You could use black and white jelly beans or black and white squares of paper instead of beads.) Place the bag at the front of the room.

Have students form a line and pass by the bag. As they pass, have them each take five beads without looking. Tell kids who have all white beads they're "perfect" and may sit down. Have the other kids go through the line again, drop their previously chosen beads back into the bag, and pick five new beads.

Have kids continue to go through the line as many as five times. Few will likely have picked five white beads.

Have kids turn to a partner and discuss these questions:

● **How easy was it to collect five white beads? Explain.**

● **How much control did you have in getting the beads you wanted?**

After the discussion, say: **The theory of reincarnation is a lot like this game. In reincarnation, people must be reborn again and again in their search to finally become perfect. How well people do in a** particular "life" determines their advantages as they start the next "round." Some people who believe in reincarnation feel bound by the actions of past lives—with little hope of escape. Ask:

● **How did you feel as you tried to get five white beads?**

Say: **Reincarnation is a popular belief within the New Age movement and Eastern religions such as Hinduism. But the Bible teaches us about a different kind of rebirth.**

Give each student a white bead. Say: **When Jesus died for our sins, he gave us the promise of resurrection. There's no "cosmic lottery" system to determine whether you'll end up with five white beads someday. God's promise is both simple and powerful: Someday, when Christ returns, believers in Christ will be given new heavenly bodies and will live eternally with Jesus. Just as you each were given one white bead as a gift, so resurrection is given to each of us as a gift from God.**

The Bible Experience

We'll Rise Again

(For this activity, you'll need Bibles, pens, treats, and a copy of the "Before You Die" handout (p. 20) for each person.)

Say: **Job suffered many terrible things in his life. Yet in the midst of his terrible suffering, he still hoped in God.** Have someone read aloud Job 19:25-27. Then ask:

● **How does Job's hope in resurrection make you feel?**

Say: **Even though Job didn't understand what the circumstances would be, he felt sure he'd see God after he died. Death is still a big unknown for us, too, because we don't fully comprehend what our new bodies will be like. But we can feel comforted knowing death won't take us farther away from God—but closer to him.**

Give each person a Bible, a pen, and a "Before You Die" handout (p. 20). This handout may bring up kids' concerns about suicide. It's not uncommon for preteens to think about suicide. If kids do bring up the issue, or if you sense kids are struggling with suicidal feelings, use this opportunity to guide kids toward positive feelings about living. Help kids see that even in the tough times, God is with them and can help them through. Encourage kids to support one another through the tough times, too.

Say: **We don't know when we'll die, but we can learn from the Bible how we can be prepared for that time. This handout will help you think about things you should know before you die. In a couple of minutes, you'll form pairs to discuss the handouts.**

After six minutes or so, have kids form pairs to discuss their handouts. During the discussion time, leave the room and bring back a cake or another treat. Then serve it to your surprised kids. Ask:

● **How did you feel as you were completing and discussing your handout?**

● **How did your mood change when you saw the treat I brought in?**

Say: **When we think about death, we often feel depressed or quiet. Yet, just as you were excited to see the treat, we'll be surprised and excited when we're resurrected and meet Jesus face to face. And the surprise will be much better than this food!**

Make a Commitment

Live It!

(For this activity, you'll need Bibles, pens, and a copy of the "Epitaphs" handout [p. 21] for each person.)

Give kids each a pen and an "Epitaphs" handout (p. 21). Say: **When our physical bodies die, we'll each probably be buried in a grave. What will your epitaph (the inscription on your gravestone) say about you? Take a couple minutes to complete the top half of your handout. Think about how people will remember you after you die. Will they remember your faith? the good things you've done for others? your joyful attitude?**

Give kids a couple of minutes; then read aloud Romans 8:10-11. Ask:

● **Does your epitaph describe a strong spiritual life? Why or why not?**

● **How can you live each day with resurrection joy?**

Form pairs. Have students read and complete the second half of the "Epitaphs" handout, tear it off, and present it to their partners.

Then form a circle. Have kids each read one thing their partners wrote about them on the handout. Then say: **We can count on God's promise of a resurrected life with him. But we can also begin to live our resurrection lives today by showing our love for God in practical ways while we have our earthly bodies.**

Have kids each tell one thing they'll do (or are doing) that can help them live resurrection lives. Kids might suggest things such as praying daily, counting on God's love, telling friends about Christ, or worshipping regularly.

New-Life Joy

(For this activity, you'll need a Bible, tape, newsprint, and a marker.)

Tape a sheet of newsprint to the wall. Have a volunteer read aloud Ephesians 2:1-5. Say: **Without Christ, we're truly dead. But when we become Christians, we gain new life in Christ and the promise of life after death—eternal life with Christ.**

Ask kids to help you rewrite Ephesians 2:1-5 on the newsprint, replacing every "you," "your," "we," and "us" with "I," "my," and "me." The rewritten passage will look something like this: "As for me, I was dead in my transgressions and sins, in which I used to live when I followed the ways of this world and of the ruler of the kingdom of the air, the spirit who is now at work in those who are disobedient. I also lived among them at one time, gratifying the cravings of my sinful nature and following its desires and thoughts. Like the rest, I was by nature an object of wrath. But because of his great love for me, God, who is rich in mercy, made me alive with Christ even when I was dead in transgression—it is by grace I have been saved."

Once kids finish rewriting the passage, close with prayer by leading kids to pray the passage to God as a "thank you" for the promise of resurrection and the joy of new life in him.

BEFORE YOU DIE

Thinking about death isn't easy for anybody. But take a few minutes to complete this handout anyway. Then find a partner, and talk about your completed handout.

- Name _____

- Age _____

- How do you think you'll die?

_____

_____

- Who will make your funeral arrangements?

_____

_____

- Who will be the most important person at your funeral?

_____

_____

- What do you want said at your funeral?

_____

_____

_____

_____

_____

- Read 2 Corinthians 5:1-9. What does this passage tell you about death? How does that make you feel about dying?

_____

_____

_____

- Read John 11:25-26. How can you count on the resurrection Jesus promised?

_____

_____

_____

_____

- Will your funeral be a joyful or sad event? Explain.

_____

_____

_____

_____

- To end this handout on a happy note, read 1 John 3:1. List two reasons you're glad to be called a child of God. Then list two reasons you're glad to be alive today!

I'm glad to be a child of God because...
1. _____
   _____
2. _____
   _____

I'm glad to be alive today because...
1. _____
   _____
2. _____
   _____

Permission to photocopy this handout from *More Smart Choices for Preteen Kids* granted for local church use.
Copyright © Group Publishing, Inc., P.O. Box 481, Loveland, CO 80539.

EPITAPHS

Part One:

What will people remember about you after you die? Write what you'd like to have written on your gravestone. Include something about your accomplishments, personality, and spiritual life.

Part Two:

What great things will your partner's epitaph say? Above, write at least two positive things your partner's gravestone might say. Think of things about his or her accomplishments, personality, and spiritual life. And remember…list only positive things!

Permission to photocopy this handout from *More Smart Choices for Preteen Kids* granted for local church use.
Copyright © Group Publishing, Inc., P.O. Box 481, Loveland, CO 80539.

Goal:

To help preteens learn what to do when they feel as if they've failed God.

Scripture Verses:

Mark 14:29-31, 66-72; John 21:15-17

Wait, God! I Didn't Mean It!

"I feel so far from God!"

This is probably not the kind of thing most preteens come right out and say. Yet many may be unsure about how to get closer to God, especially when sin and other things get in the way.

This lesson teaches kids how to draw closer to God—discovering the depth of God's forgiveness and love and trusting in God's unfailing desire to be close to them.

Opening

1-555-CALL GOD

(For this activity, you'll need a phone book and telephone.)

Say: **Let's open our meeting today by talking to God.**

Pull out a phone book and thumb through it, talking to yourself out loud: **Hear, hearts, heater...ah, there it is—heaven!** Punch the numbers on the phone as you read from the phone book: **1-555-CALL GOD.**

Say: **It's ringing.**

Say into the phone: **Hello, God? Oh, this is one of the angels. Well, this is** [your name] **from** [your church] **calling. Our group wanted to talk with God.** Pause. **I see. He's busy remodeling the Pearly Gates Bowling Alley, you say. Well, could we leave a message? Hello? Helloooo?**

To the group, say: **I was disconnected!**

Hang up the phone. Ask:

● **How did watching my phone call make you feel about God?**

● **How is that like or unlike your relationship with God in real life? Explain.**

Say: **God is always near us, but sometimes our relationship with him can feel like a "bad connection." Today we're going to talk about problems in our relationship with God and how to fix them.**

FaR FRoM GoD

Form a circle so that each person's right shoulder is toward the center. Stand in the center of the circle, and instruct students to move in as close as possible.

Say: **When a person first becomes a Christian, he or she usually feels really close to God. Let's imagine that this ring you've formed represents God. You are each as close as you can get. I'm going to read some situations. Follow the instructions as they apply to you. Be honest.**

Read these instructions slowly:

● **If you argued with anyone this week, take a step away from the center.**

● **If you seriously thought about cheating on a homework assignment or test this week, take a step away from the center.**

● **If you read your Bible every day this week, take one step closer to the center.**

● **If you talked about someone behind his or her back this week, take a step away from the center.**

● **If you prayed at least three times this week, take a step closer to the center.**

● **If you talked about your faith with a non-Christian friend this week, move one step closer to the center.**

● **If you didn't, take a step away from the center.**

Ask participants to notice how close or far from the center they ended up, then gather everyone again. Ask:

● **How did you feel when you had to admit you had done something that moved you away from God?**

● **How is this experience like your relationship with God in real life?**

● **What are other things that make you feel far from God?**

Say: **There are always things that seem to come between God and us. There was one man who was a very close friend of Jesus, and he had some problems too.**

The Bible Experience

NiGHtly NeWS RePoRt

(For this activity, you'll need Bibles, paper, and pencils.)

Form two groups. Provide each group with a Bible, paper, and pencil. Ask group 1 to look up Mark 14:29-31, 66-72, and group 2 to look up

John 21:15-17. Tell each group to read its passage and prepare a news report telling what happened. Give the groups these reporting rules:

1. The information must be accurate.

2. Everyone must be involved in the report in some way.

3. Both groups must present their reports as though they were under water.

Allow time for group preparation. Then have group 1 present its report. After the report, ask:

● **How do you think Peter felt when he realized what he'd done?**

● **Do you think it was harder for Peter to follow Christ after he made this blunder? Why or why not?**

● **When have you felt like Peter?**

● **How did you respond to God in that situation?**

Say: **In Peter's story, the way Peter dealt with God wasn't nearly as important as the way God dealt with Peter. Let's have our second report now.**

After the second report, applaud kids' efforts. Then ask:

● **How did Jesus respond to Peter's sin?**

● **What can we learn about God's ways in our own lives when we feel like we've disappointed him?**

Say: **Peter went on to be a great leader of the church. The difficulties in his relationship with God made him a stronger Christian. The disappointments we face in our relationship with God can ultimately make us into stronger Christians, too.**

Make a Commitment

Let's Get Together

(For this activity, you'll need pens and a copy of the "Let's Get Together" handout [p. 26] for each person.)

Say: **Before we look at how our disappointments can draw us closer to God, let's think about what kinds of things in our lives bring disappointment to our relationship with God.** Ask:

● **What things in our lives might make us feel as if we've disappointed God?**

● **What are ways we can please God?**

Say: **Spending time with God each day really helps us work through our disappointing times and get closer to him. Let's see how we might do that.**

Distribute a photocopy of the "Let's Get Together" handout (p. 26) and a pen to each student. Instruct kids to complete the handouts on their own. When kids have finished, have a few volunteers tell what they wrote.

Say: **Take your commitment letters home with you, and use them as a guide when you have your next get-together with God.**

Closing

Calling Again

(For this activity, you'll need a telephone.)

Pull out the phone again. Say: **We don't have a phone number for heaven. But God can hear us wherever we are, and he loves to get "calls" from us. He likes to hear our good news, bad news, thanks for the things he's done, or anything else. Keeping the communication lines open is a great way to remain close to God.**

Have each person find a partner. Tell partners each to pray, one "dialing" (opening) and the other "hanging up" (closing). Tell pairs to pray for each other's commitment to spend time with God. Also have kids each tell God one thing they're thankful for about their partners.

Let's Get Together

Complete the handout on your own.

Dear God:

Lately I feel as if things have come between you and me. A few of these things are: _____

_____

_____

_____

I would like to spend more time with you. A good time each day for me is: _____

_____

_____

It would be helpful if we could meet at the same place each day. A quiet place you could find me is: _____

_____

_____

When we are together, I'd like to talk to you about: _____

_____

_____

_____

As I read my Bible, I'll be listening for you to talk to me. I'm looking forward to our next meeting!

I love you,

Permission to photocopy this handout from *More Smart Choices for Preteen Kids* granted for local church use.
Copyright © Group Publishing, Inc., P.O. Box 481, Loveland, CO 80539.

HOPE FOR A HURTING WORLD

The preteen years are a great time to introduce kids to missions work and the possibility of spreading Christ's message to the world. Kids are old enough to plan and carry out meaningful service or outreach projects and understand the good in what they accomplish. They are open to the possibility of what their roles might be in Christ's service.

This lesson helps preteens understand that the power to share Christ comes from the Holy Spirit. And whether they can identify a call to missions or not, they can know that they all can share Christ, whether it's with a next-door neighbor or with a new friend halfway around the world.

Goal:

To show preteens that they can share their faith with others.

Scripture Verses:

Matthew 28:18-20; Acts 1:8

Opening

TELL A FRIEND

(For this activity, you'll need paper, pens or markers, newsprint and marker, and tape.)

Give each person a sheet of paper and a pen or marker. Instruct each person to draw a quarter-sized circle in the middle of the paper.

Say: **This circle represents you. Write your name inside the circle. Now imagine that you have something important to share with your friends and you tell your news to two other people. Draw an X on each side of your circle. Now imagine those two people each tell two more people. Draw two circles off each of those X's. Keep drawing two X's off each circle and two circles off each X until you run out of room on your paper.** Demonstrate this on newsprint as you explain it to kids, and then write the following numbers as you say them.

When kids fill up their papers, say: **You told two people, who told four people, who told eight people, who told sixteen people, who told thirty-two people, who told sixty-four people, who told 128 people, who told 256 people, who told 512 people, who told 1,024 people, who told 2,048 people, who told 4,096 people, and so on, and so on. You sure spread your message to a lot of people!**

NOTE

Here are some ideas to get kids started on their lists or to help them expand their lists if necessary. For missions work, they might:

- open a school,
- build a church,
- supply clothing or food,
- hold church services and Sunday school,
- supply Bibles in native languages,
- hold Bible studies,
- respond to medical or health needs,
- ease suffering from natural disasters,
- teach farming methods, or
- train native pastors and missionaries.

Christian workers might:

- help in a soup kitchen or homeless shelter;
- volunteer to help with Sunday school, vacation Bible school, or in the church nursery;
- visit or entertain at a nursing home;
- conduct a food pantry drive or clothing drive;
- help the elderly with errands or chores;
- write to a pen pal in a non-Christian country;
- correspond with missionaries from your church or denomination; or
- bring friends to church or club/class meetings.

Ask:

● **Now what could be so important that you would want that many people to know about it?**

● **If you were to share your Christian faith with all these people, what message would you tell them?**

● **If they had never heard of Jesus, what would you share with them?**

● **Do you think you could reach most of the people in the world if everyone kept the chain going and told two more people about Jesus?**

Say: **Unfortunately, there are lots of people in the world who have never heard of Jesus Christ or the Bible. And others know about him, but they choose not to believe in him or his message of love and eternal life. There are nearly six billion people in the world, and only one-third of these, or about two billion, are Christians. Let's tape our circles to the wall and think about how many people we can share our faith with, and how we might do that.**

Reflection and Application

IDENTIFYING NEEDS

(For this activity, you'll need pens and a copy of the "Reaching Out in Love" handout [p. 33] for each person.)

Say: **People who share their faith as missionaries, pastors, or church workers often have a "call" to Christian service work. A call would be sort of a summons to duty, in which you feel that God wants you to do something or you have a strong interest in doing it.** Ask:

● **How might you know if you have a call to missions or church work?**

● **What can you do to share your faith if you don't work full time in missions or church work?**

Say: **Let's form two teams. If you want to be a missionary and live in a foreign country, join the Missionary team.** Designate a gathering point. **If you want to stay in our community and help people locally, join the Christian Workers team.** Designate where this team should sit. If teams are extremely lopsided, ask a few kids to move to another team.

Distribute a "Reaching Out in Love" handout (p. 33) and a pen to each person. Tell teams they have three minutes to think of as many ways as they can to help people in their mission country or in their community. They should fill out only the top half of their handouts, brainstorming with their team members. To get kids started, you might share a few of the ideas in the "Note" list (p. 28) or give them some ideas of your own.

Then have each team demonstrate or role play its ideas to the other team. If you have time, let teams guess what's being demonstrated. Have each team fill in the ideas demonstrated by the other team on that section of the handout. At the end of this activity, each person should have the top portion of his or her handout completed.

Ask:

● **What would you most want to do if you actually got to do some of these things?**

● **What do you see on your lists that we could do as a group or as individuals right here at home?**

● **How could you share your faith while you are doing these types of service activities?**

Say: **Let's hear about a real missionary experience and learn what the Bible tells us about sharing our faith.**

The Bible Experience

Power Play

(For this activity, you'll need Bibles, a ball of yarn, and scissors.)

Say: **Listen to this true story from a missionary family in Mussoorie, India.** Read aloud the following story:

Hello from India! Greetings from Woodstock School! We are the Searles family: Douglas, Elizabeth, Mackenzie (age ten), and Mickey (age five).

We are finding that Christ's message of love, acceptance, and giving to others is so relevant to India—so needed. One aspect of life in India that takes some getting used to is the caste system. Although it was legally abolished years ago, people still feel as if they are born into a certain station in life, which determines the kind of work they may do, their potential marriage partners— almost everything important in life.

An example of the continuing effect of the caste system unfolded on the playing field here at Woodstock School. Some kids were playing soccer after school. By accident, the ball hit a man on the head, hard enough to knock him down. The kids retrieved the ball and continued playing. When staff stopped the game to ask why no one had run to the fallen man, helped him up, and apologized for the accident, the puzzled response was: "Why? He's just a bearer."

"Just a bearer." Just a low-class person who carries our heavy loads.

Imagine what your life would be like today without the under-standing that when you fall, you may be lifted up—no matter what. Imagine if Christ had not been both the bearer of good news and the bearer of everything that seems too heavy for us to carry ourselves. Lifting one another up—loving your neighbor—was a message of one of the most revered men in India, Mahatma Gandhi.

We feel called to India, and we believe that our actions here can make a difference. You, too, are being called to take action in service, in giving, and in prayer. Will you seek God's will for your life? Will you say: "Here am I, Lord; send me"?

(Story courtesy of the Searles family in Mussoorie, India, sponsored by the Board of International Ministries of American Baptist Churches/USA.)

Have kids form groups of four and read Matthew 28:18-20. Then have groups discuss these questions:

● **How is this missionary family in India doing what Christ directed in this Scripture?**

● **What kinds of problems or obstacles might this missionary family face in an unfamiliar country?**

● **Do you think it's easy to share the message of the gospel with other people? Why or why not?**

Have groups read Acts 1:8. Say: **Just as the Holy Spirit gave the apostles the power to share Christ's message throughout the world, you can receive that same power from the Holy Spirit when you ask God through prayer.** Ask:

● **What do you think the Holy Spirit's power can allow you to do?**

● **In what ways do you think missionaries and Christian workers draw on the power of the Holy Spirit?**

Have your group sit in one large circle. Hold up a ball of yarn and stretch out a strand. Say: **Look at this piece of yarn. It's not very strong by itself, is it? You could easily cut it with scissors or break it if you pulled hard enough. Think of yourself as that thin piece of yarn, and watch what we'll do to make ourselves more powerful.**

Take the ball of yarn, tie the loose end around your waist, and throw it to the person sitting directly across from you in the circle. Have that person wrap the yarn around his or her waist, and throw it to someone sitting across the circle. Instruct kids to continue until everyone is connected by the yarn. (If you have a small group, you might go around several times.)

Say: **Alone, we're weak, but together we're powerful and unbreakable! Look at the strong web we've formed, and think of how big our web could be if we each invited two more people into the circle. Now imagine asking the Holy Spirit to give you power to share your faith! We could be thousands** (point to your taped-up drawings from "Tell a Friend")**...no, we could be millions or billions of powerful Christians sharing our faith in Jesus Christ with the whole world! Let's get out of this web for the moment and think of ways we can serve God in sharing his Word.**

Have kids slip out of the yarn, or have scissors handy to cut the string around their waists.

Make a Commitment

In His Service

(For this activity, you'll need a copy of the "Reaching Out in Love" handout [p. 33] for each person, pens, newsprint, and markers.)

Have kids take their "Reaching Out in Love" handouts (p. 33) and fill in the section about talents or interests that might be appropriate in service or missionary work. You might suggest attributes such as "love to work with kids," "outgoing," "caring," "good reader," and "can play the piano."

Tell kids to take a minute to find a partner who has a same (or a similar) interest or talent and sit with that partner.

With their partners, have kids fill in the "My Commitment" section of their handouts by looking at the Christian Worker ideas at the top of the handout or thinking of another service idea they could do on their own or together as a group. Have them also fill in the "How I plan to share my faith" line. Partners may share the same ideas or help each other think of different ideas.

Gather the group, and have partners share their ideas as you write them on newsprint. Ask the group to make a commitment to do a service project as a group, and perhaps vote on which idea to pursue. Or they can commit to doing the individual projects they've listed.

Closing

Reaching Out

Say: **In the Bible, Jesus has given us our commission, or task. That is to "go and make disciples of all nations." Let me share with you a little about some of the people who have never heard of Jesus Christ or the Bible. We call these "unreached people." The Manchu people in northeastern China number more than ten million. Only about two thousand of these people are Christians.**

NOTE

Commitment to a group project might be more meaningful to your students and would help ensure that everyone participates and follows through with that commitment. To identify a good group project, evaluate the needs in your community or the needs of missionaries in your church or denomination. One interesting project could be to invite your students to become pen pals with Muslim students of the same age. Students ages eleven and older are matched with pen pals in Turkey through an organization called Turkish World Outreach. For more information write to: Turkish World Outreach, 508 Fruitvale Court, Grand Junction, CO 81504.

After your group completes its service project, be sure to have a session in which kids can share their feelings and what they learned from the project.

Traditionally, their religious practices were centered around shamanism, which means they believe there is an unseen world of many gods, demons, and ancestral spirits. Many other Manchu worship Buddha.

Or there are the Gwandara people of Nigeria in Africa. The Gwandara, who number about fifty thousand people, worship one supreme god and sacrifice goats and sheep to their god. They also have lesser gods for each village. Many Gwandara believe that they possess the power to turn themselves into hyenas. But the Gwandaras have no Christian books or films or Bibles available to them in their language. (Sources: AD2000 People Profile Index and Bethany World Prayer Center Profiles, both accessible on the Internet through Global Mapping International at http://www.gmi.org.)

Let's take a few minutes to pray that these unreached people might learn about Jesus Christ. Then pray for the commitment you made to God's service and to sharing your faith, and ask the Holy Spirit to give you the power to do these things.

Give kids a few minutes of quiet time to pray, or lead them in a prayer of your own.

Reaching Out in Love

If I were a Christian worker in my community, here's what I would do to help people:

_____

_____

_____

_____

If I were a missionary in a foreign country, here's what I would do to help people:

_____

_____

_____

_____

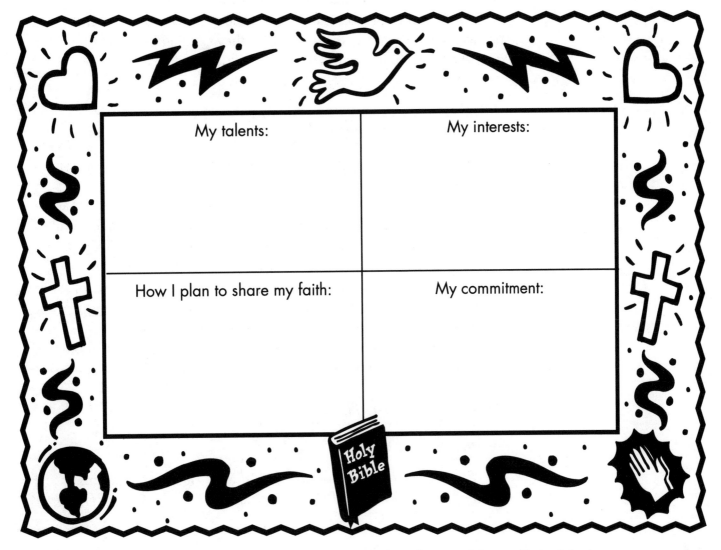

My talents:	My interests:
How I plan to share my faith:	My commitment:

Permission to photocopy this handout from *More Smart Choices for Preteen Kids* granted for local church use.
Copyright © Group Publishing, Inc., P.O. Box 481, Loveland, CO 80539.

Goal:

To help preteens find ways to overcome obstacles at school.

Scripture Verses:

Proverbs 4:23-27

ATHLETICS, ACADEMICS, and OTHER ASPIRATIONS

School. Tests are too hard; coaches are too demanding; homework is too confusing. Some kids decide to just give up and drop out, but it doesn't have to be that way.

This lesson challenges students to keep their eyes on their final goals rather than the "pain" of the moment so they can find the strength to stay on track.

Opening

WHY I MISSED THE BUS

(For this activity, you'll need paper and pencils.)

Form groups of three or four. Give each group a sheet of paper and a pencil. Tell groups to think of the ten best reasons to skip school and to provide an "excuse" for each reason. For example: Reason: Going to the beach; excuse: I was doing some research for a marine biology report.

When groups have finished, read aloud several of their reasons and excuses. Say: **As you may have guessed, today we're going to talk about school. You may feel as if everything at school goes wrong for you, but it doesn't have to be that way. Let's find out what you can do about school problems.**

Reflection and Application

WHO'S THE BEST?

(For this activity, you'll need newspaper wads, masking tape, a trash can, pens, and a copy of the "This Is a Test" handout [p. 38] for each person.)

Before the lesson make a pile of paper wads out of newspaper. Mark a free-throw line on the floor with tape that's at least ten feet from the goal—a trash can. Set out copies of the "This Is a Test" handout (p. 38) where kids can see them.

Say: **At school you spend a lot of time in the classroom. Some of you also spend a lot of time with extracurricular activities such as sports and clubs. We're going to have a little contest to see who's the best in sports and academics. You can choose either or both of the following activities to prove yourself.**

The first option is a written "test." Those who want to prove their smarts can pick up one of the "This Is a Test" handouts and complete it. The person with the most correct answers will be proclaimed Student of the Year.

The second option is a sporting event. Those who want to prove their athletic skills can form a single-file line and try to shoot paper wads into a trash can. The person with the most goals will be proclaimed Sportsperson of the Year.

After students make their choices, begin the competition. On the test, allow no cheating and no calculators! The test answers are listed in the margin.

For the sporting competition, hold the trash can in your hands and move it about so it's nearly impossible to make a goal.

Allow the competition to continue for five minutes; then regroup. Ask:

● **How did the scholars do? Any correct answers?**

● **How about the athletes? Who scored the most goals?**

● **How do you feel about this competition? Explain.**

● **Do you ever have some of these same feelings about school and school activities? Explain.**

● **What was your goal in this competition?**

● **What distractions did you face as you tried to reach your goal?**

● **Have you ever thought about what your goals are at school? What goals could you set?**

● **What kinds of distractions or disappointments do you face at school?**

Say: **It's important to know what your goals are in school. But knowing your goals doesn't mean you'll automatically reach them. Let's see what the Bible says about striving for a goal.**

The Bible Experience

DON'T DISTRACT ME

(For this activity, you'll need Bibles, newsprint, and an assortment of "distractions" such as a radio or noisemakers.)

TEST ANSWERS

1. 0.6440394
2. The judicial power of the United States, shall be vested in one Supreme Court, and in such inferior courts as the Congress may from time to time ordain and establish.
3. 1, 2, 3, 5, 8, 13, 21, 34, 55, 89
4. A special storage device used for converting time sequential information into static time parallel information.

Have the students get into groups of three to read aloud Proverbs 4:23-27. Give each group a sheet of newsprint. Say: **Read Proverbs 4:23-27, and talk about what it means to you. Then work together to tear the newsprint into a shape that represents some specific goals each of you try to strive for.**

As soon as they start, begin your special mission of distraction. Turn on a radio with loud, annoying music. Dribble a basketball around the room. Talk loudly to another leader about a movie or recent sports event. Eat raw carrots or potato chips. Ignore any rude looks or comments from the students, and continue to do everything you can to distract them.

After a few minutes, bring the group together again. Have groups show their torn newsprint and explain what they talked about. Ask:

- **Did I bother any of you?**
- **What was your goal as a group?**
- **What kept you from reaching your goal?**
- **How is that like trying to reach your goals at school?**

Say: **Let's read this passage together.**

Have someone read the Scripture aloud; then ask the students to summarize it. Say: **Reaching any goal, including goals at school, means being committed to overcoming distractions and disappointments so you can stay focused on where you're going.**

Make a Commitment

Goal Line

(For this activity, you'll need newsprint, tape, markers, a football, paper, and pens.)

Tape a large sheet of newsprint to the wall at one end of the room. Draw a huge football goal post on the newsprint. Say: **We've seen how distractions kept you from your goal of studying the Scripture passage. Now let's look at the things that keep you from your goals at school.**

Have kids brainstorm goals they have at school. Allow only answers that have to do with school and school activities—not things such as "getting a girl in your math class to notice you." Write kids' responses on the newsprint.

Say: **Let's imagine the whole room is half of a football field, with this being the goal.** Point to one end of the room. **The opposing team will be made up of all the distractions and disappointments that keep you from the goal.** Ask:

- **What are some distractions or disappointments you face when it comes to school?**

As each distraction or disappointment is named, choose a member of the group to represent that disappointment or distraction. Have these people line up on the "field" as linebackers or other football players for the opposing team. Don't let the number of disappointments exceed one-third of your group size.

Choose a student from the remaining group to be the runner who is trying to make a touchdown. Give the runner a football, and have him or her try to reach the goal without getting tagged by the opposing team.

Say: **It's hard to reach your goals with so many obstacles in the way. Now let's see how you can overcome these disappointments.**

For each disappointment or distraction represented on the field, have kids think of one way to overcome the problem. For each suggestion, select a "solution" student to stand facing the "problem" student. Try to use everyone in the group so each "problem" is surrounded.

Say: **Now let's have our runner try for the goal again.**

Run the play again, and have the solution students guard the runner all the way to the goal. Say: **Distractions and disappointments are a part of life. But with the right attitude and a few good ideas, you can press through to reach your goal.**

Form pairs, and give kids each a sheet of paper and a pen. On their paper, have kids each write one distraction or disappointment they face at school, and one way they can overcome it. Have partners exchange sheets and sign their names as "witnesses" for their partners' commitments. Then have kids each write on their partners' sheets one thing about that person that makes him or her a winner.

Say: **Keep your sheets with you at school to remind you of your goal and to encourage you when things get tough.**

Closing

PERSISTENCE PAYS

Ask:
● **How does a baby learn to walk?**
● **When Shaquille O'Neal misses a goal in basketball, what does he do?**
● **When Kristi Yamaguchi falls on the ice while skating, what does she do?**

Say: **Everyone has disappointments. If babies were to give up after falling one or two times, they would never learn to walk. If you were to give up because of a low grade, a missed shot, or some other disappointment, you would never reach your goals. Believe in God. You'll get there!**

Close with a group cheer and a final "wave."

This Is a Test

Please answer the following questions.

1. $$\frac{5(3{,}826 \times 408) + (466 \times 2{,}189)}{(82{,}251 \times 211) - (9{,}214 \times 384)}$$

2. What is the first sentence of Article III, Section 1 of the U.S. Constitution?

3. List the first ten numbers in the Fibonacci Series.

4. What is a staticizer?

Permission to photocopy this handout from *More Smart Choices for Preteen Kids* granted for local church use.
Copyright © Group Publishing, Inc., P.O. Box 481, Loveland, CO 80539.

I win, we win!

Preteens' lives are built on competition. Kids compete for grades, for athletic awards, and even for friends and dating relationships.

But abundant life is about more than competition. It's about compassion, cooperation, and love.

This lesson helps kids see life through the filter of their faith in Christ so they can learn to live by a greater standard than "looking out for number one"—a standard that places love above all, even competition.

Goal:

To help preteens recognize the value of balancing competition with cooperation.

Scripture Verses:

Ecclesiastes 4:9-12; Galatians 5:13-15

Opening

SHOE SHUFFLE

Ask kids each to take off one of their shoes. Form a circle, and have kids create a "shoe-tossing chain" with the shoes that includes everyone. (If you have more than ten kids, form two groups of tossers.) The only rule is that kids can't toss a shoe to the person directly to their right or left.

After a few minutes, have everyone stop. Ask:

● **How did you feel when all the shoes were being tossed?**

● **How is this experience like working together as a team?**

Say: **Today we're going to talk about the balance between personal competition and group cooperation. As a launch pad for our lesson, go to a person you caught shoes from, and tell him or her one thing that makes him or her a great team player.**

Reflection and Application

HUMAN TOWERS

Say: **Now let's take this team spirit one step further.**

Form groups of five or six, and have group members build a tower out of their bodies. (You may have to go outside if your ceiling is low.) Tell the groups to make their towers as tall as they can and stable enough to stand for thirty seconds. Be careful not to suggest any competition or comparison between the groups.

While the groups are building, listen for cooperative and competitive statements. When all the groups have finished their towers, congratulate each group's efforts. Have kids discuss these questions in their groups:

● How did you feel about this experience?

● How does cooperation with others help us do more?

● Did you feel that you were competing with the other groups while you built your tower? Why or why not?

● How is assuming you were competing like what happens in real life sometimes?

● How can cooperation make everyone a winner?

● How can we apply this experience to the way we handle competition and cooperation in our group?

Say: Competition can sometimes be good because it keeps us pressing on to improve ourselves. But cooperating is always good because when we work together, everyone comes out a winner.

The Bible Experience

A SYMBOL OF COOPERATION

(For this activity, you'll need Bibles, tape, newsprint, and markers.)

Form two groups. Have one group read Galatians 5:13-15. Tape a sheet of newsprint to the wall. Provide markers, and have that group work together to create a symbol that represents the Scripture passage. It's OK if the symbol has many parts, but it must be one symbol.

Have the other group read Ecclesiastes 4:9-12 and work together to create a human sculpture that represents the Scripture passage. The only rule is that every member of the group must be a part of the sculpture.

When groups are ready, have them explain their symbols or sculptures. Read aloud both Scriptures, then ask:

● What do these Scriptures have to say about cooperation versus competition?

● How was working on the symbol or creating the sculpture an example of the kind of cooperation these passages describe?

● How can we keep this kind of cooperation, even when we're competing in sports or something similar?

Say: By working together, we can do much more than we could ever do alone. And, as a group, we can act like a team all the time. Let's see how.

Penny Pals

(For this activity, you'll need pennies, construction paper, markers, glue, and tape.)

Give participants each a penny, and have them find the words "In God We Trust" on their pennies. Then ask:

● **How does this statement apply to us working as a team?**

Give each youth a sheet of construction paper and a marker. On the paper, have kids each write one way they intend to help the youth group live out the team's motto, "In God We Trust." When kids have finished, have them each tell what they wrote then sign their names at the bottom of their sheets.

Provide glue, and have kids glue their pennies on their papers; then tape all the papers to the wall of the meeting room as a testimony of cooperation.

Say: **In the days to come, let's compete to see who can cooperate the most in our group. That way, we'll help each other work toward our goal of trusting God together.**

Closing

Power Pyramid

Have the entire group go outside and create a huge human pyramid as a celebration of the team God has created the group to be. Point out that, by working together, the group members were able to build a much bigger pyramid than they did earlier in the lesson.

Close with prayer, asking God to help kids do great things as a team for him.

Goal:

To recognize when friends are in trouble.

Scripture Verses:

1 Samuel 23:16;

Ecclesiastes 4:9-12;

John 15:12-13;

Romans 12:15;

2 Corinthians 1:3-4;

Galatians 6:2

Note

Before the meeting, write the following Scriptures on a sheet of newsprint, and tape it to a wall.

1. 1 Samuel 23:16;
   John 15:12-13
2. Ecclesiastes 4:9-12
3. Romans 12:15; Galatians 6:2

KiDS in TROUBLe

The world certainly isn't what it used to be. The problems most adults faced as children are petty compared to the traumatic struggles of many preteens today. Drugs, divorce, sex, alcohol, and social pressures all take their toll on today's kids. Often kids feel alone in these struggles. But it doesn't have to be that way.

This lesson challenges kids to recognize the signs of struggle in their friends' lives—and reach out with God's love to make a difference.

Opening

inFLateD TROUBLes

(For this activity, you'll need balloons and markers.)

Have kids sit in a circle, and give each person a few balloons and a marker. Say: **I'd like you to brainstorm some problems that kids today face. Write each problem you think of on an inflated balloon, and toss the balloon into the center of the circle.**

You may need to get kids started by listing a few problems such as divorced parents or the temptation to use drugs.

After kids have finished, say: **Wow! These are some tough problems. Raise your hand if you have been affected by one of these problems personally or you know someone who has.** Ask:

● **What are some things you do when you have a problem?**

● **What are some things you do when a friend has a problem?**

Sometimes it may seem like problems like these are too big for a younger person to do anything about. But there's always something you can do. Today we're going to talk a bit about recognizing when one of your friends might be in trouble and what you can do to help.

Do You Want to Talk About It?

(For this activity, you'll need the balloons from the previous activity, paper, pencils, and an "I'm Listening" handout [p. 46] for each pair.)

Have kids form pairs, and tell each pair to choose one of the balloons in the center of the circle. Say: **The balloon you chose will represent a friend. Your friend has been affected by the problem written on the balloon. Take a few minutes to name your friend and think of some details about his or her life and the problem he or she faces.**

After a few minutes, have pairs introduce their balloon "friends" to the group. Give each person a sheet of paper and a pencil, and say: **Now, with your partner, I'd like you to think of some things your friend might say or do that might let you know he or she is in trouble. One example is a change in appetite—your friend might be eating less. Make sure that you each write the list on your own paper; you'll be taking these papers with you at the end of class.**

When pairs have finished, have them share their lists with the rest of the group. Tell kids to write down any signs of trouble that they hadn't listed before. Use the tips in the margin to finish out kids' lists.

Ask:

● **Have you ever seen any of these signs in a friend you think might be having problems? What did you do?**

Say: **The next step after recognizing a friend might be in trouble is finding a way to connect with your friend to show him or her that he or she is not alone. The best way to do this is simply to listen.**

Have pairs set aside their balloon friends. Give each pair an "I'm Listening" handout (p. 46) and a pencil.

Say: **I'd like you to take a minute to read the information about listening on the left side of the handout.**

When everyone has finished, say: **Now in your pair, I'd like you to take turns practicing really listening to each other. The person wearing the most blue will choose one of the scenarios listed on the bottom of the handout and pretend he or she is in that situation. The other person should listen to him or her using the ideas on the handout. After a minute, I'll have you switch roles. The second partner will choose another scenario.**

Give kids a few minutes to do this, and then ask:

● **How did it feel to be really listened to?**

● **How did it feel to really listen?**

● **Do you think you're a good listener? Why or why not?**

● **How do you think listening could help a person who's in trouble?**

▶ Note

This lesson may raise some sensitive issues in your kids' lives. It's possible that discussion may reveal greater problems than you feel comfortable dealing with. For more help, contact your pastor, a counselor, or one of these resource numbers:

The Bureau for At-Risk Youth
800-99YOUTH (800-999-6884)

Childhelp USA, Inc.
800-422-4453

Covenant House Nineline (a hotline for young people in trouble)
800-999-9999

▶ Signs of Trouble

● sudden outbursts of temper
● nervousness
● falling grades
● a hard time paying attention
● loss of interest in once-enjoyable activities
● withdrawal
● change in weight or appearance
● lack of appetite
● insomnia
● frequent illness

● **How is listening a part of being a good friend to someone?**

Say: **Now let's explore what the Bible has to say about being a good friend.**

The Bible Experience

A GOOD FRIEND IS...

(For this activity, you'll need Bibles, the balloons from previous activities, newsprint, markers, paper, and pencils.)

Have kids stay in their pairs, and assign each pair one set of Scriptures from the newsprint list you created before the meeting. Say: **I'd like you to retrieve your balloon friend from before. Keep your friend's problem in mind as you read your assigned Scriptures. When you've finished reading, I'd like you to decide together specific ways you could apply what you've read to your friend's situation. Then I'd like you to either create a poster storyboard or a skit to show the rest of the group what you learned and how you would help your friend according to your Scriptures.**

Provide newsprint, markers, pencils, and paper to pairs as necessary, and give them a few minutes to create their presentations. Then have pairs share their presentations with the class. Be sure that each set of Scriptures is read aloud to the class during this time. Ask:

● **According to the Bible, why is friendship important?**

● **Do you think it's difficult to be a good friend? Why or why not?**

Make a Commitment

POWER TO HELP

(For this activity, you'll need the balloons from previous activities, and markers.)

Have kids form a circle, and give each person one of the balloons created in the opening activity. Say: **Hold your balloon carefully in your hands as you think about the problem written on the balloon.** Ask:

● **How is the balloon like a person who is affected by that problem? Explain.**

Say: **These balloons are fragile and must be handled with care, just as a person who is going through a tough time needs to be handled with care. Also, these balloons are inflated, just as problems sometimes seem to be. It may seem like a friend's problem is too big to help with, and you may feel as if there's nothing you can do. But as you've experienced today, there are things you can do** to help a friend in trouble. God has given each of you special gifts and abilities that you can use to help friends in trouble.

Now I'd like each of you to write your name on the other side of your balloon. We're going to pass the balloons around the circle, and I'd like you to write on each balloon one quality each person has that would help a friend in trouble. For example, you might write "good at making people laugh" or "a good listener." Remember to be careful with the balloons.

Have kids pass the balloons around the circle until they each have their own back.

Closing

COMFORT FROM GOD

(For this activity, you'll need a Bible.)

Have kids remain in a circle. Read 2 Corinthians 1:3-4 aloud, and say: **These verses in Paul's letter to the Corinthians remind us that help and comfort come from God and that God gives us power to help and comfort others. Let's spend a few minutes silently praying for each other.**

Have kids pass their balloons around the circle one more time. As kids get a new balloon, ask them to pray silently for God to help the person named on the balloon to overcome any problems that person may be having at school, at home, or with friends. Allow about fifteen seconds for kids to pray for each person. Close the prayer after the balloons have gone full circle.

Remind kids to take their lists and handouts home with them.

I'm Listening

Read the following information, and then choose one of the scenarios to talk about.

As a good listener, you want to give your friend three important messages:

1. I'm interested in you.
2. I care about you.
3. I want to help.

To communicate these messages, follow these simple steps:

1. Find a quiet, private place to talk.
2. Sit down next to your friend.
3. Make frequent eye contact.
4. Don't criticize or judge your friend.
5. Try some active responses to encourage your friend to open up, such as "You sound unhappy," "I'm sorry you feel so bad," or "How can I help?"
6. Be yourself.

SCENARIOS

▼

Tell about your favorite relative. What makes him or her special to you?

Tell about the worst day you've ever had. What happened?

Tell about one goal you'd like to accomplish in your lifetime. Why is it important to you?

Tell about one thing this lesson has taught you. How will it change the way you deal with problems?

Permission to photocopy this handout from *More Smart Choices for Preteen Kids* granted for local church use.
Copyright © Group Publishing, Inc., P.O. Box 481, Loveland, CO 80539.

WHEN FRIENDS AND FAITH DISAGREE

T oday's young people understand diversity. The concept has been promoted in their schools since they were very young. So when it comes to making friends with non-Christians, most Christian pre- teens probably have little trouble bridging the gap. However, they also may not be ready for the internal and external conflicts that can arise when their friends and their faith disagree.

This lesson helps kids focus on the benefits and dangers of building friendships with non-Christians, and guides them to a greater under- standing of how they can effectively love their friends without compro- mising their faith.

Goal:
To relate to friends who believe differently.

Scripture Verses:
1 Corinthians 13:13;
2 Corinthians 6:14-15;
1 Peter 3:15-17

Opening
WHAT I LIKE BETTER

Have kids form one big huddle in the center of the room. Tell kids you're going to read a series of "agree/disagree" statements that you want them to respond to. Read the first statement from the "Agree/Disagree" list in the margin; then have the huddle split into two groups based on whether kids agree or disagree with the statement. Then read the second statement, and have kids break into two more groups (for a total of four groups) based on their responses. Continue reading statements and having kids divide into more groups until kids each are standing alone or in pairs.

While kids are still standing apart, say: **We all like having friends and being a part of a group. But lots of times, even disagreements over small things can separate people.** Ask:

● **What do you do when you don't agree with your friends?**

● **Has a disagreement ever ended one of your friendships? Explain.**

● **What kinds of disagreements should end friendships?**

► AGREE/ DISAGREE

1. I like strawberry ice cream more than chocolate ice cream.
2. I would rather be a teacher than a doctor.
3. I like comedies more than action-adventure films.
4. Football is more fun than baseball.
5. Going to the mall is boring.
6. I like science better than English.
7. My favorite color is red.

● What if your friends don't agree with your faith in Christ or you don't agree with theirs—should that end your friendship? Why or why not?

Say: **Today we're going to explore how we should relate to friends who believe differently. And we'll begin with an experiment that asks the question, "Can Christians and non-Christians be close friends?"**

Reflection and Application

GeT OFF MY BacK

(For this activity, you'll need tape or cloth strips.)

Form pairs, and distribute tape or cloth strips to each pair. Have the partner wearing the most white be the C partner, and the other partner be the N partner. Have partners stand back to back; then (with help from other kids) tie their arms together so that they are locked into a back-to-back position.

Once everyone is ready, give the C's this assignment: **Go to five different people, give them each a big hug, and say, "God loves you and has a wonderful plan for your life."**

After kids make the attempt, congratulate them on their efforts, and help untie them from their partner. Then have kids form groups of four to discuss these questions:

● **How did it feel to try to carry out your assignment while being tied to your partner?**

● **How might that be like trying to live for God while also trying to hang out with non-Christian friends?**

● **Do you think it's good to have close friends who don't believe in God the way you do? Why or why not?**

● **How can you be close friends with non-Christians without disobeying God?**

Say: **Friends are a blessing from God—including those friends who don't believe in God the way we do. But being friends with non-Christians is tricky because sometimes those friends can tempt us to do what's not right or to deny our faith in Jesus. Let's look more closely at what the Bible says about being friends with non-Christians.**

The Bible Experience

BewaRe BaD YoKes

(For this activity, you'll need Bibles.)

Note

In this activity and the next, C stands for Christian, and N stands for Non-Christian.

Note

Some of your kids might initially feel uncomfortable with the idea of hugging each other. Don't worry. The nature of the activity will make it difficult for any actual hugging to occur, and even if it does, the awkwardness of the situation will help add to the discussion time afterward.

Have kids stay with their partners. Have pairs read together 2 Corinthians 6:14-15. Make sure kids understand what a "yoke" is (see the note in the margin). Then have pairs discuss these questions:

● **How was being tied together in the last activity like being "yoked" in the way this passage describes?**

● **What are the dangers of being yoked to non-Christians as friends?**

● **Do you think this passage is telling us that it's wrong to have non-Christian friends? Why or why not?**

Say: **In modern times, we might describe being yoked to someone as being a partner with him or her—for example, a business partner, or a marriage partner. So the passage doesn't really say we can't be friends with non-Christians. But it does warn us to be careful in our friendships so that we don't let ourselves be pulled away from God just because our non-Christian friends don't believe as we do.**

Let's do another experiment to illustrate one other way being friends with non-Christians can be difficult.

Form two groups. Call one group the C's (for Christians) and the other group the N's (for non-Christians). Give the C's three quick servant tasks that they must do for the other group. For example, you might tell the C's to give members of the other group quick shoulder rubs, retie their shoes, or pat them on the back and say, "God loves you." Meanwhile, quietly instruct the N's to respond to each act of kindness by saying things like, "This is ridiculous," "I don't understand why you're doing this," or "Why are you doing this?"

When each group understands the instructions, have the C's perform their servant tasks. After the third act of kindness, gather everyone together and ask the C's:

● **How did you feel doing these acts of kindness?**

● **What did you think of the other group's response?**

● **The non-Christians asked you why you were doing nice things for them. If one of your non-Christian friends asked you the same question in real life, what would you tell him or her?**

● **Do you think it's hard for your non-Christian friends to understand your faith in Jesus? Why or why not?**

Read aloud 1 Peter 3:15-16, and then ask:

● **What does this passage say about being friends with non-Christians?**

● **Do you talk about your faith with your non-Christian friends? Why or why not?**

● **How can you begin to share your faith more with your friends this week?**

> ►**Note**
>
> After kids have read 2 Corinthians 6:14-15, it might be helpful to explain that a yoke is a wooden brace that farmers use to lock two oxen together side by side so the oxen can work together to pull a plow through the ground. The point Paul is making is that it doesn't make sense for two people to be yoked together if they're trying to go in two different directions in life.

Say: **Maybe we can work together to choose one way to share our faith more openly with our non-Christian friends.**

Make a Commitment

ONE WAY TO SHARE

(For this activity, you'll need Bibles, newsprint, tape, markers, pens, and a copy of the "I Will..." handout [p. 51] for each person.)

Have kids stay in two groups. Give each person a copy of the "I Will..." handout (p. 51) and a pen. Assign one group the top portion of the handout, and the other group the bottom portion. Have kids follow the instructions on the handout. While groups work on the handout, tape a sheet of newsprint to the wall.

When groups are ready, have them each call out the "I Will..." statements they created based on their assigned passage. Write kids' statements on the newsprint. After congratulating kids on their insight, say: **Now let's vote to choose just one of these statements that we'll all try to do with our non-Christian friends from now on.**

Have kids vote; then circle the statement that wins the most votes. Have kids write the statement on the back of their handouts. Then say: **Take this statement home, and think about how you can begin to do what this statement says this week.**

Closing

LOVE TRUMPS ALL

(For this activity, you'll need a Bible and pens.)

Read aloud 1 Corinthians 13:13. Then say: **Faith is important. We shouldn't hide our faith in Jesus, even when our friends don't agree. But this verse says love is greater than faith. That means we should never stop loving other people just because they don't agree with our beliefs.**

Form pairs, and have partners discuss this question:

● **How can you show love to your non-Christian friends without hiding your faith in Jesus?**

Have several pairs report what they discussed to the whole group. Then say: **God has placed his love in all of our hearts. And showing God's love to others is the most important way we can share our faith in Jesus with friends who don't know him.**

On the back of their partners' handouts, have kids write one way they see God's love shining through their partners. For example, kids might write, "You show God's love through your smile" or "You show God's love by making people laugh."

When everyone has finished, close with prayer.

I Will...

GROUP 1

Read 1 Peter 3:15; then rewrite the passage as a series of statements that each begin with the words "I will." See the example below to help you get started.

Example: "I will not become 'yoked' with non-Christians in ways that displease God" (based on 2 Corinthians 6:14-15).

I Will... _____

_____

I Will... _____

_____

I Will... _____

_____

GROUP 2

Read 1 Peter 3:16-17, then rewrite the passage as a series of statements that each begin with the words "I will." See the example below to help you get started.

Example: "I will not become 'yoked' with non-Christians in ways that displease God" (based on 2 Corinthians 6:14-15).

I Will... _____

_____

I Will... _____

_____

Permission to photocopy this handout from *More Smart Choices for Preteen Kids* granted for local church use.
Copyright © Group Publishing, Inc., P.O. Box 481, Loveland, CO 80539.

Goal:

To accept all people and cultures.

Scripture Verses:

John 4:4-10;
Galatians 3:28

Note

If you have more than twelve kids, form groups of six or fewer for this activity. That will help cut down on the length of the discussion time.

OVERCOMING PREJUDICE

We live in a strange world. People are discriminated against for ridiculous reasons, including the color of their skin, the amount of money in their bank accounts, or the countries in which they were born. Sometimes people lose their jobs, sometimes they lose their friends. And sometimes they're killed. It doesn't make sense, of course. But it really happens. And kids know it.

This lesson leads kids to explore the pain of prejudice and to discover ways they can stand against discrimination in their own school or other places they hang out. Preteens need to know that even though prejudice exists, God wants Christians to accept and love all people equally, regardless of race or culture.

Opening

UNIQUE ABOUT ME

Once everyone has arrived, form a circle. Ask kids to each think of three unique things about them that are shared by no one else in the class—their unique ethnic heritage, where they were born, or some experience they've had in life, for example. After a minute, ask kids each to share their three unique qualities with the class. Then ask:

● **How would you feel about your unique quality if people rejected you because of it?**

● **How would that experience be like prejudice in real life?**

● **What kinds of unique qualities are people rejected for in today's world?**

Say: **When you stop to think about it, it seems silly that people are rejected just because their skin is a different shade or because they were born in a different country. But, unfortunately, prejudice is a real problem in our modern world. Today we're going to talk about how we can overcome prejudice with God's help.**

52

THE MARK OF LOVE

(For this activity, you'll need watercolor markers.)

Call out three or four volunteers at random, and ask them to leave the room with an adult worker for a few minutes. Have the adult worker tell the volunteers that they're going to receive a special symbol on their cheeks that identifies them as special, unique people who are especially valuable to God and others. Then have the adult worker use watercolor markers to draw a heart shape on each of the volunteer's cheeks.

Meanwhile, instruct kids remaining in the room to ignore and avoid any physical contact with people with a heart shape on their faces. Then bring the volunteers back in the room, and lead the group in playing some easy, quick games such as Hot Potato or Duck, Duck, Goose. Pay close attention to how kids treat the volunteers and to the volunteers' reaction. Stop the games whenever the volunteers seem to be getting too frustrated or upset.

After you stop the games, form a circle and ask the volunteers:

● **How did you feel during this experience?**

Explain to the volunteers that the rest of the class was instructed to ignore people with a heart shape on their faces. Then ask:

● **How does it feel knowing that people ignored you just because of the heart shape on your cheek?**

● **How is that like prejudice?**

Ask the rest of the class:

● **How did it feel to ignore the kids with a heart shape on their faces?**

Tell the class that the volunteers were told that their heart shapes were symbols of their special value to God and others. Then ask:

● **Do you think the volunteers still feel that the heart shapes are good symbols for them to wear? Why or why not?**

● **How do you think people feel about themselves in real life when others reject them because of the color of their skin or some other unchangeable quality?**

Say: **As Christians, God wants us to accept and respect all people and all cultures equally. That's because God loves everyone equally, regardless of skin color or birthplace. Let's demonstrate the kind of love God wants us to show all people.**

The Bible Experience

celebrate uniqueness

(For this activity, you'll need Bibles and a damp cloth.)

Have the volunteers with the heart shapes on their faces sit in the center of the room, with all the other class members gathered around them. Have group members take turns telling the volunteers specific qualities that make them special and valuable as people. For example, kids might say, "You have a great personality" or "You're very smart." After several kids have shared positive qualities, provide a damp cloth so volunteers can wipe the heart shapes off their cheeks.

Read aloud John 4:4-10, and then ask:

● **How is what we just did like what Jesus did in this passage?**

● **How can you use what Jesus did in this passage as a guide for how you treat others?**

Say: **Let's come up with some specific ways we can follow Jesus' example with people we know.**

Make a Commitment

EQual Before God

(For this activity, you'll need Bibles, newsprint, tape, and markers.)

Tape a sheet of newsprint to the wall. Have kids brainstorm groups of people that kids make fun of at school or other places. Write kids' ideas on newsprint. Once you have several groups listed, have kids open their Bibles to Galatians 3:28. On "go," have kids begin to read the verse again and again in unison. As kids read, cross out the names of the groups kids identified, and then write in big letters at the top of the newsprint, "Equal Before God."

Say: **Now that we know what God expects of us as Christians, let's make a commitment together to treat all kinds of people with respect and love.**

Lead kids in the following prayer of commitment, pausing between each line to allow kids time to repeat your words. Pray:

Dear God,

Thank you for creating so many different kinds of people,

and for giving each of us unique qualities that make us special and valuable.

Because we know you want us to love all people equally,

we commit to treating others with respect and love,

regardless of the color of their skin,

where they were born,

or any other unchangeable quality that makes them unique. Help us keep this commitment from now on.

In Jesus' name, amen.

Closing

MY SPECIAL HERITAGE

(For this activity, you'll need a copy of the "My Ethnic Heritage" handout [p. 56] for each person.)

Form a circle. If kids know their ethnic heritage, have them each tell it to the class. After each person shares, have the class applaud and say, "God accepts us all as equals!" If kids don't know their ethnic heritage, have them name an ethnic group they like, such as American Indians or Eskimos.

Before dismissing the class, give each person a copy of the "My Ethnic Heritage" handout (p. 56). Say: **Each of us has a unique ethnic heritage. It's one of the things that makes us special as individuals. Ask your parents to help you fill out this handout so you can learn more about your own unique ethnic heritage.**

My Ethnic Heritage

Ask your parents to help you answer each of the questions below.

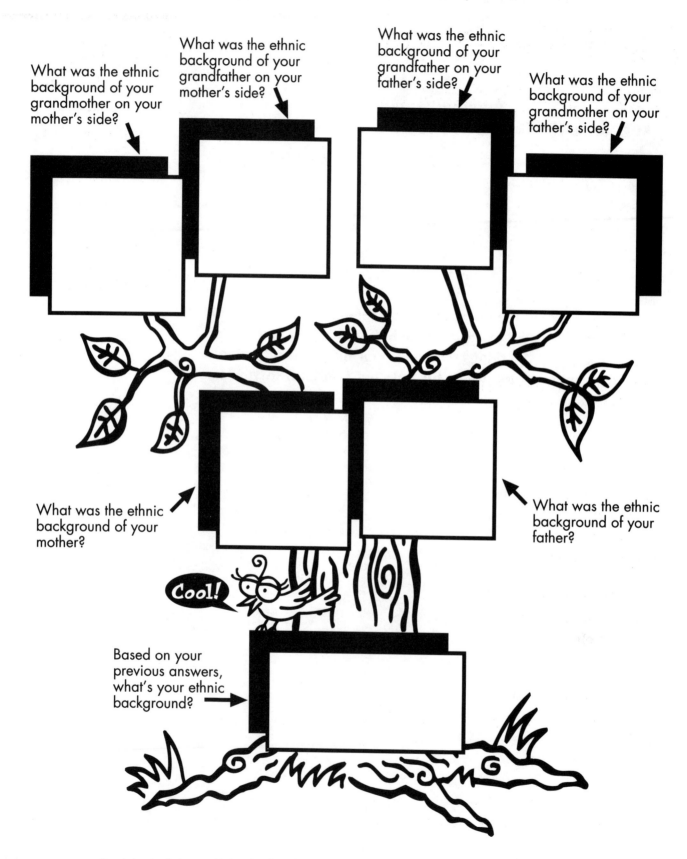

What was the ethnic background of your grandmother on your mother's side?

What was the ethnic background of your grandfather on your mother's side?

What was the ethnic background of your grandfather on your father's side?

What was the ethnic background of your grandmother on your father's side?

What was the ethnic background of your mother?

What was the ethnic background of your father?

Cool!

Based on your previous answers, what's your ethnic background?

Permission to photocopy this handout from *More Smart Choices for Preteen Kids* granted for local church use.
Copyright © Group Publishing, Inc., P.O. Box 481, Loveland, CO 80539.

FRiCTiON iN THE FAMiLY

Goal:
....
To help preteens discover healthy ways to deal with family problems.

A home can be a challenging place. All preteen kids, whether they're from intact families or single-parent homes or blended families, experience disappointment at home at various times. Sometimes kids may even feel their homes are nothing more than battle-grounds.

This lesson teaches kids that there are ways they can improve life at home—even when they find themselves in situations that are beyond their control.

Scripture Verses:
....
Genesis 37:1-28

Opening
....

KEEPiNG HOUSE RELAY

(For this activity, you'll need paper sacks, copies of "The Relay Instructions" [p. 58], aprons, articles of clothing, spoons, jars of baby food, cans of vegetables, and makeup.)

Have kids form "families" of four; then have family members number off from one to four. For each family you'll need a sack containing the following items: one copy of "The Relay Instructions," an apron, any article of clothing, a spoon, a jar of baby food, a can of vegetables, and any kind of makeup (lipstick or eye shadow will do).

Say: **Today we're going to talk about our families. To help us get that at-home feeling, I've divided you into family units. This relay will help us determine which family has it all together.**

Hand each family a paper sack and a photocopy of "The Relay Instructions" (p. 58). Say: **Go!**

Monitor the families to be sure each person does his or her designated task. Also be sure that the apron is worn, not just tossed along to the next person.

Congratulate the first- and second-place families for being such good role models for the community.

Say: **I hope our home lives aren't too much like this. But even if you don't have to eat baby food for dinner, there may be other** areas where your home life is failing. Today we're going to talk about dealing with disappointments at home.

Reflection and Application

FAMILY FEUDS

(For this activity, you'll need Bibles, pens, and copies of the "Secret Snags" handout [p. 61] and "Family Feuds" handout [p. 62] for each "family.")

Before the lesson, photocopy the "Secret Snags" handout (p. 61), and cut it into the designated sections. For larger groups photocopy the sheet as many times as needed.

Give each family a photocopy of the "Family Feuds" handout (p. 62), a pen, and a Bible.

Say: **I'd like to give each family a chance to prove its knowledge of the Bible. Before we begin, I'll give each person a "secret snag" that will help or hinder your family. Be sure to keep it a secret from everyone in your family, and be sure to do exactly what the paper says.**

THE RELAY INSTRUCTIONS

1. Your spouse will be home for dinner soon, and the house is a wreck! **Number 1:** Put on the apron, get the article of clothing, and run to the bathroom to wash it and wring it out. After you return with the clean laundry, pass the apron to **Number 2,** who must put it on.

2. It's time to feed the baby! **Number 2:** Get the spoon and baby food, and feed **Number 3** three spoonfuls of his or her delicious dinner. Pass the apron to **Number 4.**

3. Time to make dinner. **Number 4:** Get out the veggies, and set them on the floor. Pass the apron to **Number 1.**

4. Are you looking your best for your honey? Better freshen up your makeup! **Number 1:** Put on the makeup. Do a good job! Pass the apron to **Number 2.**

5. Your honey is home! Give him or her a kiss on the cheek, and eat a romantic dinner together. **Number 2:** Kiss **Number 3** on the cheek, and sit down for dinner. Then pass the apron on to **Number 4.**

6. The food looks good, but you haven't said your prayer. **Number 4:** Say a prayer to bless the food; then dig right in. Yum! Yum!

Permission to photocopy these instructions from *More Smart Choices for Preteen Kids* granted for local church use. Copyright © Group Publishing, Inc., P.O. Box 481, Loveland, CO 80539.

Hand out the secret snag slips, and allow students to look only at their own. Then have families start work on their "Family Feuds" handouts.

When the families have finished, have kids read their secret snags to their families. Have families discuss these questions:

● **What went wrong in your family?**

● **How did you feel as these things happened? Explain.**

● **How are these situations and feelings like problems in your own homes?**

● **How did you feel if you were a troublemaker? Explain.**

● **How did you feel if you were trying to make peace and finish the activity?**

● **Did any of the secret snags remind you of yourself? Why or why not?**

● **What other things cause disappointment in families?**

Say: **We all experienced disappointment in our families just now, but disappointment in real-life families can be devastating. Let's check out a fellow in the Bible whose family was full of disappointment.**

The Bible Experience

What to Do About Joseph

(For this activity, you'll need Bibles, markers, and newsprint.)

Have someone read aloud Genesis 37:1-2. Say: **OK, tell me what you know so far about Joseph.** List kids' responses on newsprint.

Say: **Here is a little more information about Joseph. He was one of twelve brothers who were from the same father and four different mothers. To add to this, none of the mothers got along. Some of your own family situations may remind you of this!**

Ask someone to read aloud Genesis 37:3-10. Say: **Using the information we have gathered from these verses, I'd like each family to pretend Joseph is one of the brothers in your family. What is your family going to do about Joseph? And what does your family think Joseph should do?**

Give the families several minutes to discuss the situation and decide on their actions. Have each family briefly tell the whole group its plan to improve things.

Say: **Now that we've given our solutions, let's see what really happened.**

Read aloud Genesis 37:11-28. Ask:

● **How did your solutions compare to what really happened?**

Say: **This situation may sound dismal for Joseph, but God turned it around for good. Years later, Joseph was given a high** position in the Egyptian government and saved his family from starving to death during a seven-year famine. And none of this would have happened if he'd never gone to Egypt as a slave.

Make a Commitment

HEART FOR HOME

(For this activity, you'll need newsprint, marker, tape, red paper, scissors, and pens.)

On a sheet of newsprint, draw an outline of a house, and tape the newsprint to the wall. Give kids each a sheet of red paper and scissors, and have them each cut out four heart shapes.

Say: **God turned things around for Joseph and made a bad situation turn out well. When things go wrong in your home, it may be hard for you to see how God could turn it around for good. But he can, if you'll let him help you.**

I may be able to help too. When things are beyond your control and you feel that you want out, it may be best to talk to me, a youth leader, or an adult you trust. Whatever the situation, God can help make it better. But you have to take the first step.

Hand out pens. Ask kids to think of four ways they can improve things in their own home, and write each of those things on a separate heart. Have kids tape the hearts inside the house outline.

Say: **Even when things go wrong in our homes, there's almost always something we can offer to help the situation. Before we close, regroup with your family, and tell each person one quality he or she has that can help make a great family!**

Closing

FAMILY TIES

(For this activity, you'll need yarn.)

Set up a start line and a finish line for a quick race. Have students gather again in their families at the start line. Tie a piece of yarn around each family. Explain that the family that makes it across the finish line first (with the yarn still tied) will be declared the ultimate Family of the World.

Congratulate the winning family, and then say: **Our real families are tied together by bonds too. By drawing closer together and cooperating, as you did in this race, you can help your family reach its goal. Let's remember that each of us can help to make our own homes better places to live.**

Close with prayer, asking God to help kids overcome disappointments at home.

secret snags

Photocopy and cut apart these instructions as indicated.

You are too cool for this activity.
Ignore everyone in your family.

Make everyone happy.
Agree with all the others
even if they're wrong.

Do your best to help your family
cooperate.

Argue with all the others even if you
think they may be right.

Make fun of every answer given by the
person sitting to your right.

Hog the Bible, and don't let anyone help
you look up the verses.

This is such a boring activity. Be sure
everyone knows how bored you are.

Be as helpful as possible so your family
will do its best.

Turn your chair around and face the
opposite direction. You can participate;
just don't look at anyone.

Try to cheat by sneaking over to the other
teams and glancing at their answers.

Cooperate and try to get everyone in
your family to work together.

Brag about how easy this is and how
anyone who doesn't understand isn't
as smart as you.

Keep changing the subject. Talk about
the weather, your clothes, sports,
television—anything but the activity.

Try to get everyone to work together to
help your family come in first!

Complain about how unfair this
activity is.

Encourage family members to do
their best.

Don't agree with anything said by the
person sitting to your left.

Threaten to leave the group if everyone
doesn't work together and win.

Listen and smile, but don't offer any help
in getting this done.

Keep poking the people sitting next to
you with your elbows.

Permission to photocopy this handout from *More Smart Choices for Preteen Kids* granted for local church use.
Copyright © Group Publishing, Inc., P.O. Box 481, Loveland, CO 80539.

Family Feuds

Find the Scripture reference that matches each Bible headline.

_____ **MAN KILLS ONLY BROTHER**

_____ *Man finds out he has been tricked into marrying the wrong woman*

_____ **Godly priest is found to have evil sons**

_____ ***WOMAN RAPED BY HER HALF-BROTHER***

_____ **King marries seven hundred women; problems sure to follow**

_____ Man claims his beautiful wife is his sister

_____ *Queen kills entire family to preserve her place on the throne; one baby secretly saved*

_____ **BROTHER SELLS HIS INHERITANCE FOR A QUICK MEAL**

_____ Letter to church offers advice to kids and their parents

_____ *Widow poses as a prostitute in order to become pregnant by her father-in-law*

_____ *Two sisters who want children get their father drunk so he will sleep with them*

- Genesis 25:29-34
- Genesis 19:30-36
- 2 Samuel 13:1, 12-14
- Genesis 4:8-9
- 1 Samuel 2:12
- Ephesians 6:1-4
- 1 Kings 11:3
- 2 Kings 11:1-3
- Genesis 38:15-19
- Genesis 12:11-13
- Genesis 29:21-25

Permission to photocopy this handout from *More Smart Choices for Preteen Kids* granted for local church use.
Copyright © Group Publishing, Inc., P.O. Box 481, Loveland, CO 80539.

LIVING WITH ONE PARENT

Goal:

To understand how God values and helps all families.

Scripture Verses:

Deuteronomy 10:18;

Psalm 68:5;

Proverbs 17:6;

Ephesians 6:1;

Colossians 3:20

With the many pressures, temptations, and opportunities kids face today, parenting preteens can be tough. But the job of raising children becomes doubly hard for parents who lose a spouse to divorce or death. Those parents, in particular, need all the help they can get.

This lesson focuses on helping kids see how they can lend a hand to their single parents, not just by doing their chores, but also by praying for their parents on a regular basis. That's because kids' prayers may be the best help a parent can ever hope to receive.

Opening

BALANCING ACTS

(For this activity, you'll need balloons.)

Form pairs, and give each pair a handful of balloons. Have each person blow up one balloon to represent each person in his or her family. Then have partners work as a team to try to keep all of their balloons in the air at once.

After thirty seconds, stop the action and say: **Running a family is a real balancing act. But just imagine what happens when one parent leaves the scene.**

Have the partner wearing the most white step aside; then tell the other partner to try to keep all the balloons aloft by himself or herself. After thirty seconds, stop the action, and let the other partner give it a try. Then stop the action again, and ask pairs to discuss these questions:

● **What made this activity difficult?**

● **Let's say these balloons represent children in a family. How is trying to keep them all in the air by yourself like being a single parent?**

Say: **Being a parent is tough in any circumstance. But it's doubly hard if you're a single parent. Today we're going to explore how we can help our parents—especially single parents—do their job.**

> ## NOTE
>
> Although some of your kids won't be from single-parent homes, you can still help them apply the lessons from this study by encouraging them to focus on ways they can help both of their parents do their jobs more effectively.

Reflection and Application

One-Eyed Dream Weaver

(For this activity, you'll need newsprint, markers, masking tape, string, and scissors.)

Have kids help you place newsprint on all the walls. Then provide markers, and have kids each pick a space on the newsprint. Tell kids to think of one great dream for themselves that they want to come true when they grow up. For example, some kids might want to become doctors, dancers, or professional athletes. Tell kids you want them each to draw a picture of their dreams on the newsprint. Before they begin, however, distribute string and have kids each tie their dominant hands to the feet on the same sides of their bodies. (Encourage kids to help each other accomplish this.) Then distribute masking tape, and have kids each tear off a small piece of newsprint and tape it over their right eyes as an eye patch. Then let kids make their drawings.

When the drawings are complete, have kids each turn to a partner and explain their drawings. Then have kids help untie each other. Gather kids and ask:

● **What did you think of this experience?**

● **Why was it so hard to draw your dream?**

● **How is losing the use of part of your body in this task like losing a husband or a wife in the task of raising kids?**

Say: **All parents want their children's dreams to come true. But single parents have a harder time providing their children with the support they need to achieve their dreams. That's why it's so important for young people to do all they can to help their parents succeed. This is especially true for those who have single parents.**

The Bible Experience

Help List For Single Parents

(For this activity, you'll need Bibles, pens, and a copy of the "Help List for Single Parents" handout [p. 66] for each person.)

Form two groups, and give each person a pen and a copy of the "Help List for Single Parents" handout (p. 66). Assign each group a different section of the handout, and have kids work together with their group members to complete it.

When groups have completed the handout, have groups take turns leading the class in their prayers for single parents. After the prayers, say: **Offering these prayers for single parents is good. But the truth is that single parents need our prayers all the time. Let's**

Note

If you have more than twelve kids, it's OK to form into several small groups for this activity. Then at the end of the activity, have groups take turns leading the class in their prayers for single parents.

hear from some real-life single parents so we can learn more about how to pray for them every week.

Make a Commitment

PRAYER PROMISES

(For this activity, you'll need newsprint, tape, and markers.)

Before the lesson, ask a few single parents to join your class for this portion of the lesson. Tell them you'll have the kids ask them a few questions so kids can learn how to pray more effectively for their own single parents. Then, before the parents enter, write each of these questions on a separate sheet of paper:

- What's the hardest thing about being a single parent?
- What's one easy way kids can help their single parents every week?
- What would you like people to pray for you as a single parent?

Distribute the questions to individuals in the class. Tape a sheet of newsprint to the wall. Then invite the single parents to join you. Have kids with questions take turns asking them, and allow each single parent to respond. Then allow kids to ask any additional questions they may have. Write all the parents' responses on the newsprint.

After the question-and-answer time, thank the parents for coming, and let them leave. Then guide kids to review the parents' answers that you recorded on the newsprint. Based on parents' responses, ask students each to name one thing they will pray for their own single parents or another single parent they know.

Say: **We've gained many ideas for ways we can help our parents do their job more easily. But no matter what else we do, it's important to remember that praying for your parents regularly is probably the best thing you can do for them.**

Closing

PARENTAL THANK YOUS

(For this activity, you'll need a Bible, newsprint, tape, and markers.)

Place a sheet of newsprint on the floor. Across the middle, write the second part of Proverbs 17:6, which says, "parents are the pride of their children." Then have kids brainstorm things they're thankful for about their single parents or other single parents they know. As a closing, have kids write their "thank yous" on the newsprint. Then have kids take the newsprint to the church foyer and tape it to a wall so everyone can see it. Encourage kids to tell their parents to read it.

Then dismiss the class.

▶ **Note**

To avoid embarrassment, it may be best to choose single parents who don't have kids in your class.

HELP LiST FOR SiNGLe Parents

GROUP 1

1 Read together Ephesians 6:1 and Colossians 3:20.

2 Based on the passages, create a list of things kids can do to lend a hand to their single (or married) parents. Write that list here:

_____

_____

_____

_____

3 Based on the list you created, write a short prayer to God asking him to help you do these things for your parents. Write your prayer here:

_____

_____

_____

_____

GROUP 2

1 Read together Deuteronomy 10:18 and Psalm 68:5.

2 Based on the passages, create a list of things God will do to lend a hand to kids with single parents. Write your list here:

_____

_____

_____

_____

3 Based on the list you created, write a short prayer to God asking him to do the things he promises in the Scriptures you read. Write your prayer here:

_____

_____

_____

_____

HELP LiST FOR SiNGLe Parents

Permission to photocopy this handout from *More Smart Choices for Preteen Kids* granted for local church use.
Copyright © Group Publishing, Inc., P.O. Box 481, Loveland, CO 80539.

A Parent's Perspective

Goal:
....
To understand parents' roles in kids' lives.

Scripture Verses:
....
Deuteronomy 11:19-21; Ephesians 6:1-2

With any sports team, winning is the goal, and teams win when all the players know and play their positions. A quarterback may be able to pass the ball, but if there is no one to block the rushers, fake out the defenders, or run the correct pattern, he won't complete the play.

Kids need to know that the family is more than just a haphazard group of people, it's a team. And like a team, each member wins when all the family members know their positions and their roles.

This lesson shows kids that God has designed the family to work together as a team and helps them discover their own "winning" role within the home.

Opening
....

PARENT FOR A DAY

(For this activity, you'll need index cards and pens.)

Distribute index cards and pens; then say: **If you could ask or say anything to your parents, what would it be? Write your response on the card you've been given. I want to read what you write to the entire group. Do not sign your name. I will collect the cards when everyone has finished.**

When you have collected the cards, shuffle them and read them to the class. After each card has been read, ask:

● **If you were a parent, how would you respond to this situation?**
After you have read all the cards, ask:

● **How did it feel to play the role of your parent?**

● **How would your parent respond if you asked these questions?**

● **What's the worst thing that might happen if you asked these questions?**

● **What's the best thing that might happen if you asked these questions?**

Say: **Playing a role sometimes helps us get an idea of what**

> ## Note
> If some kids respond to these questions with flippant, smart aleck answers, go ahead and laugh along, but move the kids past that answer to more serious responses. Sometimes a flippant remark is for a laugh, but sometimes it's a good indicator that you're touching a sensitive area.

someone else is supposed to do. But those ideas are just *our* ideas. In his Word, God has an idea or two for families. Today we're going to talk about the roles we're each called to play within our families.

Reflection and Application

PRIME TIME FAMILIES

(For this activity, you'll need newsprint, tape, markers, a box of assorted props for role playing parent-preteen scenarios, and one or more copies of the "Scenarios" handout [p. 71] cut apart, so you have a situation for each pair of participants.)

Form pairs. Tape a sheet of newsprint to the wall. Ask kids to brainstorm a list of fictional families they have seen on television. As they suggest names of families, assign a number to each one. Then say: **You and a partner will role play a situation. One of you will act out the role of a parent, and the other person will act out the role of the young person. I have written your TV families' names on the wall and numbered them. I'll hand you a situation any family might encounter, and your twosome will present it as if you're one of the TV families. You can choose the family, but I'll assign the situation. You will have a few moments to "get your act together" and come out acting.** Give a different situation from the "Scenarios" handout (p. 71) to each pair.

Once kids are prepared, start the scenes. Continue until every pair has had a chance to role play. Then have groups discuss these questions. Ask:

● **How did it feel to act out your situation as if you were a TV family?**

● **How is playing a role in this activity like the way we each play a role in our real families?**

● **Would you like to be in a TV family rather than a real family? Why or why not?**

● **If you were a writer for a TV family, how could you make the programs more true to life?**

Say: **Being in a TV family means always knowing what to say and when to say it. Real-life families don't have the advantage of scriptwriters, but we do have direction from God's Word to help us relate to our family members in healthy, loving ways. Let's take a look at a few of those biblical directives.**

See and Do

(For this activity, you'll need Bibles, red and blue markers, a light prop that won't hurt anyone if thrown, newsprint, and tape.)

Before class write the words of Deuteronomy 11:19-21 and Ephesians 6:1-2 on newsprint. Tape the newsprint to the wall.

Say: **In the Bible, God has given many examples of what a family should be and even more guidance to parents. Today we are going to explore two Scriptures that apply to the team we call the family.**

Have the students circle the action verb of each responsibility described in the Scriptures on the newsprint. Use a blue marker for the child and a red marker for the parents. When all the action words have been identified, ask:

● **What surprises you about these words?**

● **What do the verbs in these verses reveal about your role in your relationship with your parents?**

Pick up a light prop and say: **Every action must have a reaction. If I throw this prop to [name a student], he or she will catch it. My throwing is an action; catching it is a reaction. Next to the action words on the newsprint, let's use the appropriate marker to list the reactions that would be appropriate to each action. For example, if parents are to teach, what should the reaction of the child be?**

Ask volunteers to call out an appropriate reaction to each of the action words. Then ask:

● **How would you rate your parents on their actions and reactions as you have listed them on the newsprint?**

● **How would you rate yourself on your actions and reactions as you have listed them on the newsprint?**

● **What does it mean to honor your parents?**

● **Is it always easy to honor your parents? Why or why not?**

Say: **Sometimes people go to the doctor to get well, and they get prescriptions they don't especially like. The medicine may taste bad, or they might have to quit doing something they love to do. When you go to the doctor, you have to follow his or her orders to benefit from his or her wisdom. The same principles are in effect when it comes to God's Word. It's time to do what the doctor has prescribed.**

Make a Commitment

IS HONOR EARNED OR GIVEN?

(For this activity, you'll need a sticker, a trophy, or a certificate — anything that denotes honor or success. You'll also need index cards, pens, and a piece of newsprint and a marker for every two people.)

Have kids form pairs, and give each pair a piece of newsprint and a marker. Say: **Think about what it means to honor your parents.** Display the trophy or certificate, and say: **In today's society, people get trophies, certificates, and awards when they are being honored. How can you honor your parents? Work in pairs to find ways to honor your parents, and then list them on the newsprint.**

When pairs have finished, have them place their newsprint on the floor so everyone can see it. Say: **Let's go through the ideas you've presented and cross out the duplicates.**

As you read each idea aloud, have kids cross out any ideas that have already been mentioned and, at the end of the exercise, circle the ideas that aren't duplicates. Once the lists have been narrowed, ask:

- **How many of these ways of honoring your parents are realistic?**
- **What is keeping you from honoring your parents?**
- **How can you put one of these ideas into action?**

Give an index card and a pen to each person. On the card, have students each write the following commitment, pulling specific ideas from your discussion: "I will honor my parents by [list the honoring activity], and I will have this accomplished by [date]. I understand that God has given my parents a specific role and has led me to honor them."

When kids have finished, say: **You've seen the roles that God has given to each member of the family, and you've worked on a commitment. Now you need support from the rest of our team.**

Closing

SHARE AND DECLARE YOUR INTENTIONS

(For this activity, you'll need the index cards from the previous activity.)

Say: **Honoring your parents can be tough. It sometimes takes courage and resolution. God has commanded us to honor our parents, and we've set a goal to do so. Remember, God never commands us to do something that he isn't willing to assist us in doing. You also have the support of the people in this class.**

Re-form student pairs, and have kids share with each other the goals they have written on their cards. Have partners pray for each other while they both hold the note. End with a large group prayer, asking God to help kids keep their commitment to honor their parents and to help parents be strong in the roles that God has established for them.

★ SCENARIOS ★

You are out two hours beyond your curfew, and your parents meet you at the door.

You want to go to a movie that your parents are not excited about. You are rushing out the door when your parents ask, "Where are you going?"

Your parents "assume" that you will baby-sit your younger brother or sister without asking you. Your mom breaks the news to you as your parents walk out the door.

It's report card time, and the results are not the best. Your dad asks about the report card.

You have just broken up with your "special someone," and your mom asks about it. Does she care, or is she just being nosy?

Permission to photocopy this handout from *More Smart Choices for Preteen Kids* granted for local church use.
Copyright © Group Publishing, Inc., P.O. Box 481, Loveland, CO 80539.

LOVING BROTHERS AND SISTERS

Goal:

To get along with siblings.

Scripture Verses:

Genesis 25:27-34; 27:30-36

"Stop touching me! Mom, will you tell him to stop touching me?" Most of us remember those funny lines from comedian Bill Cosby, as he talked about the struggles young children face in getting along with each other. Unfortunately, as kids grow older, they don't always get better at getting along. Sometimes they need a little encouragement to learn how to love each other better.

This lesson guides kids to examine their own relationships with their brothers and sisters and to consider ways they can foster an "alliance" with their siblings that will last not just for a day, but for a lifetime.

Opening

STICK FIGURE FAMILIES

(For this activity, you'll need paper and pencils.)

Once everyone has arrived, form a circle, and give kids paper and pencils. Ask kids each to draw a stick figure family portrait. Have kids include each family member's name on the portrait; then have kids write a one-line description of each family member. Here is an example: "Dad—he's a truck driver who's only home on weekends."

When everyone has finished, have kids share their family portraits with the class. Then say: **Every family is unique—we each have unique blessings and unique struggles in the families we've been given. Today we're going to talk about the special struggles that come with trying to get along with brothers and sisters.**

Reflection and Application

THE AVOIDER, THE BORROWER, AND THE NAG

Form trios. Have each trio member choose one of these roles: the Borrower, the Nag, and the Avoider. Tell kids the Avoider's goal is to get as far away from the Borrower and the Nag as possible, without leaving

Note

Some of the kids in your class may not have any brothers or sisters. If so, include them in the activities and discussions by phrasing the questions to include getting along with parents or close friends.

In addition, many of your kids may have stepbrothers or step-sisters in addition to their other siblings. For the purposes of this lesson, encourage kids to think of getting along with step-sib-lings in the same way they think of getting along with their full siblings.

the room. The Borrower's goal is to stay close to the Avoider and try to borrow anything he or she can—a shoe, a Bible, or anything else in the Avoider's possession. Meanwhile, the Nag's goal is to stay close to the Avoider and boss him or her around with commands such as "Don't go over there! Stand here and talk to us!" and "Give the Borrower what she wants!"

Once everyone understands his or her role, start the game and allow it to continue for a few minutes. Then stop the game, and have trios discuss these questions:

- **What's your reaction to this experience?**
- **Did you like your role? Why or why not?**
- **Which character are you most like in your family?**
- **Which characters are most like your siblings?**
- **How was this activity like living with brothers and sisters in real life?**
- **What's the best way to deal with siblings when they avoid you, boss you around, or try to borrow stuff from you?**

Say: **The Bible tells a real-life story of two brothers who didn't get along. They didn't like each other, and their whole relationship was full of trickery and disrespect. Let's take a closer look at what happened to these brothers to see if we can learn any lessons that might apply to our own family relationships.**

The Bible Experience

I've Got a Beef With You

(For this activity, you'll need Bibles, scrap paper, pens, and a copy of the "Beefs Against Brothers" handout [p. 76] for each person.)

Form two groups, and name one group Esau, and the other group Jacob. Distribute scrap paper, pens, and copies of the "Beefs Against Brothers" handout (p. 76). Have groups complete their assigned portions of the handout.

When kids have finished, say: **Now that you have a stack of "beefs" against your brother, let's use them to attack each other.**

Have kids take one or more of the grievances they wrote on scrap paper and crumple them up to form paper wads. Draw an imaginary line down the center of the room; then have each group line up in a pyramid shape on either side of the line, facing each other. (See the diagram in the margin.)

Say: **Most (or all) of you have one or more paper-wad "beefs" to hurl at your opponent. Before we begin, let me tell you the rules. You can throw only those paper wads you are holding. You may not move from where you are standing to avoid a paper wad,**

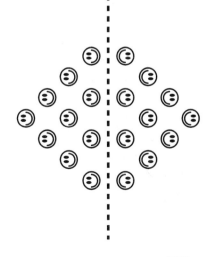

> ### Note
> If you have more than twenty-four kids, have kids form four groups instead of two for this part of the lesson.

but you may duck to avoid being hit. If you are hit, you are considered "dead" and must sit down on the floor. The contest is over when all the paper wads have been thrown once. The winner will be the team with the most people left standing.

Once kids understand the rules, start the game. After the game, have kids each find a partner from the opposing team; then have pairs discuss these questions:

● **How did it feel to try to hurl your beefs without getting hit yourself?**

● **How is this activity like the way Jacob and Esau treated each other?**

● **How is this activity like the way you and your siblings treat each other?**

● **What's wrong with treating each other like this?**

● **How should Jacob and Esau have treated each other? Why?**

● **How should we treat our brothers and sisters? Why?**

After the discussion, say: **Even though getting along with brothers and sisters can be hard, with a little kindness, they can quickly become your greatest allies. Let's find out how.**

Make a Commitment

ALLIED FORCES

(For this activity, you'll need newsprint, tape, marker, paper, and pens.)

Have kids stay in pairs, and give each pair a sheet of paper and a pen. Have kids work with their partners to come up with a list of ways they'd like their siblings to be their allies in life. For example, kids might write, "I wish my brother would play sports with me" or "I wish my sister would help me clean up the kitchen more often."

While pairs work, tape a sheet of newsprint to the wall. Once each pair has listed two or three ideas, have kids share their ideas with the class. Write kids' ideas on the newsprint. When the list is complete, say: **To gain an ally, you have to be an ally. We've created a great list of ways we wish our siblings would be allies to us. But now let's turn it around and look at this list as ways that we can be allies to our brothers and sisters.**

Have kids each choose one or two ideas that they like best and commit to doing those things for their siblings this week. Have kids write the ideas on scrap paper so they don't forget. Then say: **If you keep doing things like these for your brothers and sisters, it won't be long before they begin to do some of the same things for you.**

ALLIED PRAYERS

Have kids re-form their trios from the Reflection and Application activity, "The Avoider, the Borrower, and the Nag." Say: **Today you pretended to be brothers and sisters who couldn't get along. Now let's pray together for our real brothers and sisters. Let's ask God to help us be friends with our siblings and support them in ways that please God.**

Have trio members each say a one-sentence prayer for each of their partners, asking God to help them get along with their siblings.

After the prayers, dismiss the class.

Beefs Against Brothers

Complete your group's section of the handout.

Esau
GROUP

Read together Genesis 25:27-34; 27:30-36. As you read, put yourself in Esau's place. Think about all the reasons Esau might be angry with Jacob. Then work together to brainstorm a list of all the grievances or "beefs" that Esau might have against Jacob. (The more beefs you can think of, the better!) Then write each beef on a separate piece of scrap paper.

When you've finished, raise your hand and wait for the leader's instructions.

Jacob
GROUP

Read together Genesis 25:27-34; 27:30-36. As you read, put yourself in Jacob's place. Think about all the reasons Jacob might not like Esau. Then, work together to brainstorm a list of all the grievances or "beefs" that Jacob might have against Esau. (The more beefs you can think of, the better!) Then write each beef on a separate piece of scrap paper.

When you've finished, raise your hand and wait for the leader's instructions.

Permission to photocopy this handout from *More Smart Choices for Preteen Kids* granted for local church use.
Copyright © Group Publishing, Inc., P.O. Box 481, Loveland, CO 80539.

KeePinG THe FamiLY Lines oPen

Goal:

To help kids to communicate better with their parents.

Scripture Verses:

Deuteronomy 11:18-21

Parents of preteens often feel they've lost importance in their kids' lives. Doors that were once open slide shut as kids seek privacy and independence and as friends become tremendously important—sometimes more important than Mom and Dad.

The result: Family communications close down just when they're needed most. It would be great if parents were always willing and able to work through the barriers and reopen lines of communication. But parents' feelings get hurt, too. They give up hope. They draw into themselves to protect their feelings.

The good news: Parents are only half of the relationship. *Preteens* can open up lines of communication too. This lesson helps kids discover how.

Opening

QUICK-SKeTCH RaLPHie

(For this activity, you'll need paper and a pencil with an eraser for each person.)

Give a piece of paper and a pencil with an eraser to each student. Say: **In the days before photography was common, newspapers used to keep quick-sketch artists on staff. Their job was to quickly draw a picture of what was described to them. They were fast and often had to use their imaginations to fill in the details.**

Congratulations: You're now all quick-sketch artists at the National Gazette. I'm going to tell you a story about someone named Ralphie. As I do, quickly draw Ralphie. Draw *one* portrait of Ralphie—you'll simply update it with details as I continue my story.

Remember: Don't worry about drawing a perfect portrait. It's

more important to the National Gazette that you work in the details. Ready?

Tell the following story, pausing as indicated.

Ralphie was a beautiful baby—cuddly, chubby, and cute (pause fifteen seconds). **Ralphie had a dimple on his left cheek when he smiled** (pause five seconds), **but he hardly ever smiled. Ralphie liked to play with a rattle, which he held in his right hand** (pause five seconds). **He had chunky little thighs that slimmed down when he started to walk. Ralphie loved to walk** (pause five seconds). **He walked every day until he started to run. Then he ran everywhere he went, wearing his favorite T-shirt and shorts** (pause ten seconds). **Soon he was riding a bicycle** (pause ten seconds), **but not before he rode a tricycle** (pause five seconds). **On his bicycle Ralphie waved at everyone he saw** (pause ten seconds). **He was such a friendly kid. He was friendly in elementary school, where he wore little high-top sneakers** (pause ten seconds), **and in middle school, where he wore big, thick glasses** (pause five seconds), **and in high school, where he got rid of the glasses and wore contact lenses** (pause ten seconds) **and a mustache** (pause five seconds).

After the story, ask students to compare their sketches. Say: **Whew! Keeping up with Ralphie was a challenge! He changed so fast! And if I asked your parents, they'd say keeping up with you as you grow and change is a challenge, too.**

Here's a tip: You can help your parents keep up by talking with them and telling them what's going on in your life. They probably want to know what you're thinking. But if you count on your parents to read your mind, you'll be disappointed. You've got to *talk* with them.

Form pairs, and ask partners to discuss these questions:

● **Was it hard to keep up with me as you created the drawing? Why or why not?**

● **How is that like it might feel for your parents as they watch you grow up?**

● **How do you feel when you can't keep up with something that changes quickly? Explain.**

● **How is that like how your parents might feel about keeping up with you?**

Say: **In the same way you can feel frustrated when things change quickly in your life, your parents can feel lost or frustrated when you change so fast. Your feelings and your parents' feelings are just two obstacles that can come between you and your parents. Let's uncover others with this next activity.**

COMMUNICATION BLOCKERS

(For this activity you'll need newsprint, markers, pencils, tape, strips of paper, a soft foam ball, and empty soda cans.)

Have kids form pairs. Distribute two strips of paper, two empty soda cans, tape, and two pencils to each pair. Say: **Lots of things keep kids from connecting and communicating with parents. For instance, if your parents are always at work, you won't communicate much.**

Ask pairs to discuss:

● **What's one thing that keeps you from connecting with your parents? Explain.**

When pairs have shared, ask each student to write the thing he or she identified on a slip of paper. Then ask students each to tape their strips of paper to an empty can. As kids work, write "SCORE!" on a small sheet of newsprint, and spread it out on the floor next to a wall.

When kids have finished, arrange the empty cans into a wall in front of the "Score" newsprint. Create an imaginary line on the floor ten feet from where you've placed the cans. Have kids take turns rolling a foam ball through the cans to try to reach the "Score" newsprint. Reset the cans after each roll.

When all students have had a turn, ask them to take their seats. Ask:

● **In this game, was it always easy to score? Why or why not?**

● **How did it feel to have to get past the wall to reach the "Score" base?**

● **How is trying to break through the cans like trying to break through communication barriers in your family?**

Say: **Let's find out how many of these problems would be knocked down—or at least helped—if parents and kids were listening and talking to each other. As I read what's written on each can, lean to your right if you think communication would help. Lean to your left if you think communication wouldn't help at all.**

Read what's written on each of the cans, and have kids lean left or right depending on their opinion. Arrange the cans into two piles according to kids' responses.

When you've finished, say: **Keeping communication lines with parents open makes a difference. Most of your conflicts with parents will be helped or eliminated if you do.**

And it's not just your parents' job to keep communication lines open. It's *your* job, too. We'll talk about how you can help make that happen.

▶ **Note**

If you use tin cans rather than soda cans, warn students that the rough edges at the top of empty cans might cut fingers. Ask students to be careful, but to guarantee safety, cover rough edges with duct tape.

The Bible Experience

Location, Location, Location

(For this activity you'll need a Bible, a white board or a chalkboard, newsprint, tape, and a marker.)

Tape a sheet of newsprint to the wall. Ask your students to sit in chairs or on the floor in a circle around you.

Read Deuteronomy 11:18-21 aloud, one phrase at a time. Instruct your students to leap to their feet every time they hear a place or time parents are instructed to talk with their kids. Keep track of the locations on a white board or chalkboard.

Quickly review the results; then form five groups. (If you have fewer than five students, do this activity as one group.) Assign one of the following situations to each group: sitting at home, walking along the road, lying down, getting up, and passing through door posts and gates (at home).

Ask each group to brainstorm at least two inexpensive ways kids can talk with their parents about important things in each of these situations. For example, one way to talk while lying down is to have a family camp-out or a slumber party in the living room.

Give groups one minute to come up with their ideas. Ask each group to report its ideas to the larger group. Summarize the ideas on the newsprint.

When reports are finished, have kids form pairs. Ask students to select one idea on the board that they'd like to try at home. Then ask students to discuss the following questions in their pairs:

- **Why did you pick the idea you selected?**
- **What would you talk with your parents about there?**
- **How would it feel to talk with your parents more?**

Make a Commitment

Chat Date

(For this activity you'll need pens and a copy of the "Invitation" handout [p. 82] for each person.)

Working in pairs, ask students to create an invitation to their parents to actually implement the idea they've identified. Distribute pens and copies of the "Invitation" handout (p. 82) to each person. Have kids complete their invitations. Then have them share their invitations with their partners. Ask kids to pray for each other, asking God to help them follow through in giving their invitations to their parents.

If at all practical, use cell phones, pay phones, or the local church phone to let students make brief phone calls to actually invite their parents immediately. This guarantees the invitations will actually be offered—and the paper invitations can serve as a reminder.

Closing

PARENT PRAYERS

(For this activity, you'll need the empty soda cans from the earlier activity.)

Ask each student to pick up one of the empty soda cans and then stand in a circle. Say: **Opening lines of communication with your parents can begin with you. It means you've got to listen and you've got to share what you think and feel. If you do, you'll see how good communication smashes lots of problems.**

I want us to pray for your "chat dates" with your parents. But before we do, please place your cans on the floor. Let's smash these communication problems and then ask God to smash the problems we might have communicating with our parents.

Place a can on the floor, and then place your foot on the can and crush it. Encourage your kids to do the same.

When you've crushed the empty cans, open a time of prayer for kids to pray for their parents and for better communication in their families.

INVITATION

Date: _____

From: _____

To: _____

You are cordially invited to:

_____

At this date and time:

_____

For this reason:

_____

Signed:

_____

Permission to photocopy this handout from *More Smart Choices for Preteen Kids* granted for local church use.
Copyright © Group Publishing, Inc., P.O. Box 481, Loveland, CO 80539.

WHOSE WORLD IS IT ANYWAY?

P reteens know the Creation story. But they need encouragement to accept the responsibility of caring for God's creation. A generation of young teenagers can have a substantial impact on improving environmental quality.

This lesson challenges your preteens to care more deeply for the earth.

Goal:

To help preteens accept responsibility as care-takers of the earth.

Scripture Verses:

Genesis 1:28-30; 2:15; Psalm 8

Opening

FIRE DRILL

(For this activity, you'll need a trash can, index cards, and markers.)

Form a circle around a metal trash can. Give each person a marker and a few index cards. Say: **Imagine for a moment that the house next door is on fire. You've been given two minutes to evacuate your home. In that time, what will you rescue from your house? We'll assume all your family members and pets are safe, so choose other things to save. To save something, write a description of it on an index card, and toss it into the trash can. You must also write your name on each card. You have two minutes.**

Give kids two minutes to list as many things as possible. Then call time. Pour out the cards that were tossed into the trash can. Have volunteers read aloud what people wrote. Ask:

● **How did you feel having only two minutes to save things from your house?**

● **How did this limited time affect what you wrote on your cards?**

● **How did you decide what to save?**

Say: **If this had been a real fire, you'd want to save yourself and your family members before all material goods. Still, we each have things we'd not want to lose in a fire. As in this activity, we'd try to save certain items. Our lesson today is about saving something. And it's about taking care of something we should value—our earth. We each have a responsibility to take care of God's creation.**

I CREATED THAT

(For this activity, you'll need paper and crayons.)

Give each person a sheet of paper and crayons. Have kids each find a place in the room away from others. Say: **In this activity, you're going to use crayons to create a beautiful scene from nature. Draw exactly what I tell you, and don't look at anyone else's work. I'll be giving you a number of instructions, so try to keep up.**

Don't worry if you think you can't draw. Your effort is more important than your skill. Your completed pictures will be given as an offering to God, so do your best work.

Read aloud the following directions, allowing one-minute intervals between each:

● **Draw land on your paper. Add some water if you'd like. You have one minute.**

● **Draw the sky. Put birds, clouds, and the sun in your sky. You have one minute.**

● **Add flowers, trees, and animals to your drawing. You have one minute.**

● **Add people to your picture. You have one minute.**

Gather the group in a circle. Go around the circle, asking people to hold up their drawings so the group can see them. Collect all the drawings.

Set the drawings in front of you and, one at a time, tear them up as the students watch. Don't say anything. Throw the resulting pile of paper into the center of the circle.

Student reaction at this point will be mixed. Allow a moment for kids to evaluate your actions. Then ask:

● **How did my actions make you feel?**

● **How is that like the way God must feel when he sees us destroy his world?**

● **How do people destroy the world we live in?**

Say: **God loved us so much he gave us a beautiful planet to live on. All we had to do was take care of it. God promised that the earth would provide everything we need to be healthy and happy.**

Now we're in trouble. We've hurt our earth with pollution and practices such as deforestation. And if these practices continue, the earth will not be able to provide for our needs.

God gave us this world as a beautiful gift to take care of. We, as Christians, should take responsibility for caring for this gift. Everything we do to care for our planet sends a love letter to God.

CaRetakeRS

(For this activity, you'll need Bibles.)

Form groups of no more than four, and give each group a Bible. Have each group meet in a separate area of the room. Assign each group one of the following verses: Genesis 1:28; Genesis 1:29; Genesis 1:30; and Genesis 2:15.

Say: **These verses from Genesis tell us that God gave us the responsibility to care for the earth. God entrusted his creation to us. It's something we all must take seriously.**

In your group, read aloud your verse. Then decide on four or five ways you can care for the earth according to the command in your verse. For example, you might decide you can care for the plants by planting trees in your neighborhood.

Choose one or two of your ideas, and design short pantomimes of the ideas for the other groups to guess. For example, if your idea is to pick up litter, your group could act that out.

Allow five minutes for groups to brainstorm ideas and determine which ideas they'll pantomime. Then bring the groups together. Have them take turns pantomiming their ideas for the other groups to guess. Ask:

● **How did you decide on the things your group pantomimed?**
● **Why do people sometimes not want to care for God's earth?**
● **What are ways we can help make the earth a better place?**

Make a Commitment

MY ReSPONSiBiLitY

(For this activity, you'll need a copy of the "Taking Care of the Earth" handout [p. 87] and a pen for each person.)

Give kids each a "Taking Care of the Earth" handout (p. 87) and a pen. Say: **This handout lists a few of the major problems facing our planet. Carefully read your handout and complete it honestly. After you've finished, form pairs to discuss the ideas on your handouts.**

Use the ideas in the "Ways to Care" list (p. 86) to help kids come up with ideas for the handout.

After students complete the handouts, form pairs. Have partners discuss the questions on the handouts. Then have students read the commitment at the bottom of the handout, complete it, and read it aloud

ways to care

- Car pool often.
- Ride bicycles or walk whenever possible.
- Report pollution concerns to local authorities.
- Avoid using plastic foam products.
- Recycle paper, glass, and plastic products.
- Conserve water.
- Reuse products when possible.
- Buy products that are biodegradable or packaged in biodegradable materials.

to their partners. Have partners sign each other's commitment as witnesses. Have kids report back to the whole group what they learned about taking care of the earth.

Then form a circle. Have kids shake hands with at least three other people, thanking them for committing to caring for God's creation. Say: **Even the smallest effort will help God's world. Just imagine if what you've committed to do were multiplied by a million. With God's help it could happen.**

Closing

PSALM 8

(For this activity, you'll need a Bible.)

Have kids sit in a circle. Have kids repeat after you as you read Psalm 8, one line at a time. Vary your voice inflection to dramatically convey the meaning of each verse, and have kids copy your voice inflections. Afterward, ask students how reading this psalm made them feel. Close by having volunteers thank God in prayer for the wonders of the world he has given us.

TAKING CARE OF THE EARTH

This handout lists a few of the major problems facing our earth. Read each problem carefully. Then, if you feel you can do something to help solve this problem, complete the sentence.

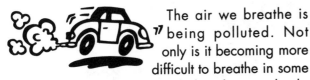 The air we breathe is being polluted. Not only is it becoming more difficult to breathe in some areas, our skies are turning dark with smog thanks to automobile exhaust and pollutants from factory smokestacks and other sources.

● I could help solve this problem by...

_____

_____

The ozone layer in our atmosphere protects us from dangerous ultraviolet rays from the sun. That layer is being destroyed by dangerous CFCs (chloro-fluorocarbons released from the manufacture of products such as plastic foam containers).

● I could help solve this problem by...

_____

_____

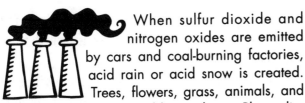 When sulfur dioxide and nitrogen oxides are emitted by cars and coal-burning factories, acid rain or acid snow is created. Trees, flowers, grass, animals, and people are being covered by acid rain. Plants die. Water is poisoned.

● I could help solve this problem by...

_____

_____

_____

People have carelessly used oil, trees, and water with little effort at conservation, and we're using up these natural resources.

● I could help solve this problem by...

_____

_____

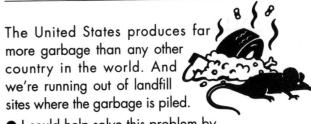 The United States produces far more garbage than any other country in the world. And we're running out of landfill sites where the garbage is piled.

● I could help solve this problem by...

_____

_____

Discuss the following questions with your partner:

● How do you feel about these environmental issues?
● How do you feel about your responses to these issues?

Complete the commitment below by filling in at least one of your suggestions above.
Then go out and show people how to care for God's creation!

I hereby commit to _____
to help save the earth God has given us as a gift.

Signed: _____

Witnessed by: _____

Date: _____

Permission to photocopy this handout from *More Smart Choices for Preteen Kids* granted for local church use.
Copyright © Group Publishing, Inc., P.O. Box 481, Loveland, CO 80539.

Goal:

To help preteens recognize and know how to respond to the lure of drugs and drinking.

Scripture Verses:

Matthew 4:1-10;
1 Corinthians 6:19-20;
10:12-13;
Hebrews 11:24-26;
James 1:13-15

THE LURE OF SUBSTANCE

Kids face the lure of drugs and alcohol too frequently in our society. Movies, television, and music publicly glamorize drugs and drinking. And school friends offer kids drugs and alcohol. It's a dangerous temptation for kids. And one that often brings deadly results.

This lesson helps preteens understand that, just like a fishing lure, the lure of drugs and alcohol has a painful—and potentially deadly—hook hidden in it.

Opening

THE DOUGHNUT

(For this activity, you'll need doughnuts.)

Form pairs. Give each pair one doughnut. Say: **Imagine for a moment that these doughnuts are a new illegal drug, said to give a great feeling to anyone who eats them.**

Have partners alternately take thirty seconds to try to convince each other to take a bite of the doughnut. Tell kids they can use any tactic they want to convince their partners of the value of eating the doughnut. They may choose to give in or not.

● **Were you tempted to eat the doughnut? Why or why not?**

● **How did you feel as your partner tried to convince you to eat the doughnut?**

● **How is that like the feeling some people have when tempted to take drugs or drink alcohol? Explain.**

● **How easy was it to keep from eating the doughnut? Explain.**

● **How was the temptation to eat the doughnut like the temptation to take drugs or drink alcohol?**

Say: **We're constantly bombarded by temptations. Many things seem good but really may be bad. People say drugs and alcohol will make you feel better—but unlike the doughnut, they actually can do great harm. Today we'll talk about the risks and dangers of drugs and drinking.**

Have students eat their doughnuts.

RISKY BUSINESS

(For this activity, you'll need masking tape, paper plates, dried beans, newsprint, and markers.)

Use masking tape to make a long, straight line on the floor. Have kids line up at one end of the masking tape line. Give kids each a paper plate, and have kids hold the plates upside down on the palms of their hands. Pour about one-quarter cup of dried beans onto each person's plate. Then have kids walk the straight line without spilling the beans. Ask:

● **Was it easy to walk the line without spilling the beans? Why or why not?**

Next, have kids line up again behind one end of the masking tape line. Spin the first person in line seven times. Then have him or her immediately attempt to walk the line again without spilling the beans. Repeat with each person in line. When everyone has attempted to walk the line a second time, ask:

● **Was it easy to walk the line this time? Why or why not?**

● **How did you feel as you tried to walk the line the second time?**

● **What made walking the straight line the second time more risky than walking it the first time?**

● **How is trying to keep from spilling the beans while walking this line like taking a risk?**

On a sheet of newsprint, write, "What makes a risk a risk?" Have kids brainstorm things that make activities risky, such as potential danger or lack of control of a situation. Write these on the newsprint. Then have kids call out risky behaviors such as sky diving, skateboarding, telling a stranger about Jesus, playing sports, taking drugs, and skiing. List these on the newsprint. Have kids vote on the items they think are "smart" risks and those they think are not-so-smart risks. Have someone circle the items the group thinks are smart and place an X through those they think are not so smart.

● **What's the difference between a smart risk and a not-so-smart risk?**

● **When you take a risk, how do you feel?**

Say: **Using drugs and alcohol is risky. The thrill of taking a risk is enough temptation for some people to try something. But just as being spun around took away your ability to walk straight, drugs and drinking can take away your control and put you at great risk.**

Yet drugs and drinking remain a great temptation for preteens. The temptation to seek pleasure isn't new.

Look up Hebrews 11:24-26 and read it aloud. Say: **In Bible times, many people faced temptations. Fortunately, just as people such as Jesus and Moses could beat temptation, we can beat temptation too.**

The Bible Experience

AVOIDING THE LURE

(For this activity, you'll need Bibles, pens, and a copy of the "Strength From the Word" handout [p. 93] for each person.)

Say: **Millions of people have used illegal drugs at least once. It takes a strong person to stand against the temptations of drugs and alcohol. And God wants you to be one of those strong people.**

Give each person a Bible. Form two groups. Have one group read Satan's lines and the other group read Jesus' lines in Matthew 4:1-10. Have a volunteer read the narration. Ask:

● **What were Jesus' temptations?**
● **How did Jesus respond?**

Read Hebrews 11:24-26 again. Ask:

● **What temptation did Moses face?**
● **How did he respond to that temptation?**
● **What do Jesus' and Moses' examples teach us about dealing with the temptations of drugs and alcohol?**

Give each person a "Strength From the Word" handout (p. 93) and a pen. Have kids complete their handouts.

Afterward, form pairs. Have partners each share their completed handouts. Then have pairs each decide one thing they can do to help friends overcome the lure of drugs and alcohol. Have each pair pantomime its idea for the rest of the class to guess. For example, a pair might pantomime someone removing a drink from a friend's hand. Ask:

● **How important is it to seek God's help when you're tempted by the lure of drugs and alcohol? Explain.**

● **How can these Scriptures help you stay strong and avoid the lure of drugs and alcohol?**

Say: **Much of the lure of drugs and drinking is based on lies. And when we can see the lies, it becomes easier to resist the temptation.**

Make a Commitment

CHAIN REACTION

(For this activity, you'll need paper slips, pencils, and tape.)

Distribute 1x4-inch paper slips, pencils, and tape to students. Say: **The things that tempt us can become the things that hold us captive. On the slips of paper, write things people tell you to convince you to use drugs or alcohol. For example, you might write, "It'll make you feel good" or "You won't get caught."**

Have each person complete two or three slips. Then have kids form a paper chain using the slips and tape. After the chain is formed, have kids take turns sharing what they wrote. Ask:

● **How do you feel when you hear someone use one of these lines?**

● **How many of the lines are really lies?**

● **How is the lure of drugs and alcohol like the chain we just made?**

● **How can we break the chain of lies?**

Say: **With God's guidance and each other's support, we can expose these lies and break the temptation of drugs and drinking.**

Have each person tear one or two links of the paper chain. Then form pairs. Have partners share how they feel about the temptation of drugs and drinking. For example, someone might say, "I'm confident I can beat the temptation" or "I still feel nervous about being offered drugs or alcohol." Then have kids promise each other they'll do all they can in the upcoming week to avoid the lure of drugs and drinking. Have kids tell their partners which positive qualities they have that can break the chain of lies—confidence, solid faith, and a sense of humor, for example.

Encourage kids to keep a torn link from the chain as a reminder that they can overcome the lure of drugs and alcohol.

Closing

BOWL OF IDEAS

(For this activity, you'll need dried beans from the "Risky Business" activity and a bowl.)

Form a circle, and give each person a dried bean from the "Risky Business" activity. Say: **I'm going to go around the circle with a bowl. As I pass by you, place your bean in the bowl and say one thing you can do to avoid the lure of drugs and alcohol. You might want to say something you learned from the Scripture passages we read or something you learned in your group.**

Kids might say, "I can trust God to help me beat the temptation" or "I know my friends can help me stay strong."

Beginning with yourself, go around the circle collecting the beans.

Say: **In our earlier activity, we used paper plates to carry the beans. But paper plates are flimsy. Sometimes we may feel flimsy too as we face difficult temptations of drugs and drinking. But with God's assurance and the insights from Scripture, we can become less like a flimsy plate and more like this solid bowl as we face the lure of drugs and drinking.**

Close in prayer, asking God to help kids overcome the lure of drugs and drinking.

Strength
FROM THE
Word

Read James 1:13-15; 1 Corinthians 6:19-20; and 1 Corinthians 10:12-13. Then, based on those passages, complete the handout.

Summarize what the passages tell you about facing the temptations of drugs and alcohol.

_____

_____

_____

_____

_____

_____

Draw a picture representing how you feel, knowing God can help you overcome temptation.

Draw a picture representing how you feel when tempted to do things you don't believe are right.

What can you learn from these passages to help you overcome the lure of drugs and drinking?

_____

_____

_____

How can you use the message of these passages to help friends overcome the lure of drugs and drinking?

_____

_____

_____

Permission to photocopy this handout from *More Smart Choices for Preteen Kids* granted for local church use.
Copyright © Group Publishing, Inc., P.O. Box 481, Loveland, CO 80539.

Goal:

To help preteens develop reasons for caring about school.

Scripture Verses:

Genesis 37:5-11;
Psalm 143:8-10;
Proverbs 10:13-14; 23:12

WHO CARES ABOUT SCHOOL?

"Why do we have to learn all this stuff? We'll never use any of it anyway."

Ever hear that one before? Students today live so much in the "now" their future seems too far away to worry about.

This lesson gives kids positive reasons for caring about school by helping them to see how an education will help them fulfill their own dreams and God's plan in their lives.

Opening

SCHOOL VOTE

(For this activity, you'll need newsprint, tape, and a marker.)

Say: **Imagine our elected officials decided to let students choose whether they want to attend school. Let's imagine they drafted a law stating kids could decide to stop attending school once they finished the fourth grade. But a majority vote would be required to allow the law to be passed.**

In a couple of minutes, you'll each get to vote on the law. But first, you'll each get to say what you think is good or bad about requiring kids to attend school.

Go around the room and have kids each say one thing they like or dislike about being required to attend school.

Then tape a sheet of newsprint to the wall, and draw a vertical line down the middle. On the left side, write, "Let Students Choose," and on the right side, write, "Require Students to Attend."

Have kids take turns walking up to the newsprint and signing their names in either column, depending on how they vote. Total the number of names in each column, and declare the new law as accepted or rejected depending on the votes.

When everyone has signed the newsprint, ask:

● **How did you feel about the way you voted?**

● **How is that like the way some people feel about attending school?**

● Was there any pressure to vote a particular way? Explain.

● Would you vote differently if this were a real law being presented by our elected officials? Explain.

Say: **While you may like the possibility of choosing whether to attend school, you must for now, anyway, go to school. But school doesn't have to be something you dread — in fact, school can help you accomplish goals in life. Today we'll explore how.**

Reflection and Application

Planning Ahead

(For this activity, you'll need tape, paper, pens, and a copy of the "Wanna Be" handout [p. 99] for each person.)

Form groups of no more than four. Give each group tape and fifteen sheets of paper. Say: **The object of this activity is to use all the paper you've been given to create a sculpture that is easily recognizable. You may tear, roll, fold, and tape the paper any way you'd like. You'll have three minutes to create your sculpture. But here's the catch — you may not talk or write notes to each other during this activity.**

After three minutes, call time. Have groups guess each other's sculpture. Then give each group another supply of paper, and say: **Now you'll do the same activity, but you'll have one minute to plan before beginning your sculpture.**

When one minute is up, call time and say: **Now, for the next three minutes, you may not talk or write notes. Based only on your planning discussion, complete your project.**

After three minutes, call time and have groups display their complete sculptures. Ask groups to guess each other's sculpture. Then form a circle, and place all the sculptures in the center of the circle. Ask:

● **How easy was it to complete your sculpture the first time?**

● **How did you feel as you tried to work together on this project without planning first?**

● **How is that like the way people feel when they don't reach a goal in life because of poor planning?**

● **How much easier was it to create a sculpture when you planned ahead of time? Explain.**

● **How important was planning in this activity?**

● **How is the importance of planning in this activity like the importance of planning to reach goals in real life?**

● **How is education a part of planning for life?**

Say: **Without training and planning, you can easily feel lost or without direction. But by exploring different areas of knowledge in school, you're each given a picture of possibilities for the** future. **You also discover the first steps toward being what you "wanna be."**

Give kids each a photocopy of the "Wanna Be" handout (p. 99) and a pen. Have kids complete the handouts. Then form a circle, and have volunteers tell what they wrote on their handouts. Be sure to support and affirm kids' comments. Ask:

● **In all of these dreams, what role does learning play?**

Say: **If you think of going to school as a chore and a waste of time, it will be both. But if you think of going to school as an opportunity to prepare for your future, it can be fun. And since school can help you reach your potential and meet your goals, it can also be extremely valuable.**

The Bible Experience

THE GREAT-POTENTIAL AWARD

(For this activity, you'll need Bibles.)

Form groups of no more than four. Read aloud Genesis 37:5-11. Have kids take turns completing the following sentence in their groups: "If I were Joseph, I'd feel _____ because _____."

Say: **Now take turns telling each other about a dream you've had for your future. After each person tells about his or her dream, everyone else must say something positive and supportive to that person. For example, you might say, "You've got a great dream—go for it" or "I know you can reach this goal."**

Then form a circle. Say: **If a "Great-Potential Award" were given to a Bible character, it would probably go to Joseph. He, like each of you, had dreams of accomplishing something in his life. But sometimes friends and family members can't see the same dreams God has for our lives.**

One of the reasons people don't believe in your dreams is because they only see who you are now and can't see how your future will develop. Joseph didn't immediately see God's plan for his leadership come true—it took time and hard work. God wants you to prepare now so you can fulfill your dreams and God's plans in your life. And school is an important part of that preparation.

Have everyone stand at one end of the room against a wall. Read aloud Proverbs 10:13-14 and Proverbs 23:12. Then ask the following questions. Each time someone calls out an idea, have everyone take one step forward. Kids might suggest ideas such as, "by helping us learn what we do well" or "by helping us learn new skills." Ask:

● **What do these verses say about education?**

● Why does the Bible encourage us to seek knowledge?

● How can school help you reach your potential?

After a few ideas have been suggested, say: **Look how far you've come away from the wall. Just as each idea took you one step closer to the other end of the room, each idea can help you reach your potential and your dreams. School can help each of you reach for your Great-Potential Award.**

Make a Commitment

WHY I CARE ABOUT SCHOOL

(For this activity, you'll need a pen and a copy of the "Why I Care" handout [p. 100] for each person.)

Give each person a photocopy of the "Why I Care" handout (p. 100) and a pen. Allow five minutes for kids each to complete the handout.

Then form pairs. Have partners tell how they felt completing the handout. Encourage partners to discuss each other's handout if they feel comfortable doing so. Then have kids tell their partners one thing they'll change about the way they view school. Remind students to decide on positive changes.

Form a circle, and have volunteers tell what changes they're going to make concerning school. Stay in circle formation for the closing.

Closing

TEACH ME, OH LORD

(For this activity, you'll need a Bible.)

Form a circle. Say: **Your teachers at school may be great or not so great, but education is important either way. Thankfully, we always have one teacher who is great—Jesus. I'm going to read aloud a Scripture passage. Before I do, I want each of you to kneel and hold your hands up toward the ceiling. Then repeat each phrase after me. This will be our prayer.**

Read aloud Psalm 143:8-10. Pause after each phrase to allow kids to repeat the phrase after you. After the prayer, have kids stand. Then ask:

● **How did it feel to pray in this position?**

● **How does this position reflect a teachable attitude before God?**

● **Why is it important to look to God as your teacher and leader in life?**

Say: **Each time you pray this week, raise your hands to God as a reminder to yourself to follow God's teaching in every aspect of your life.**

Wanna Be

Remember all the things you said as a child about what you wanted to be when you grew up? Now's your chance to list those dreams to help you see how far you've come.

In each of the boxes, list one of your dreams about what you'd like to do in the future. Begin with things you wanted when you were younger, and work up the stairs until you complete the top box, which will describe your current dreams. For example, if you used to think it would be fun to be a firefighter, complete the first box accordingly. Use the sample below to guide you.

Sample:

When I was **seven**, I wanted to be a **firefighter** just like **my dad** because **I thought it looked like fun.**

When I was _____

I wanted to be a _____

just like _____

_____

because _____

_____

When I was _____

I wanted to be a _____

just like _____

_____

because _____

_____

When I was _____

I wanted to be a _____

just like _____

_____

because _____

_____

I WANNA BE...

Permission to photocopy this handout from *More Smart Choices for Preteen Kids* granted for local church use. Copyright © Group Publishing, Inc., P.O. Box 481, Loveland, CO 80539.

WHY I CARE

Why should you care about school? What makes education worth all the hard work? Below, list five benefits of education, and answer the questions.

Why education is important:

① _____

② _____

③ _____

④ _____

⑤ _____

? Was it easy to think of benefits of school? Explain.

? Based on the Scripture passages read earlier, what importance do you think God places on your education?

? What do these benefits tell you about the value of school?

? How do you think school fits into God's plan for your life?

Permission to photocopy this handout from *More Smart Choices for Preteen Kids* granted for local church use.
Copyright © Group Publishing, Inc., P.O. Box 481, Loveland, CO 80539.

Pagan Practices

Goal:
To help kids understand what evil is and how Christians discern good from evil.

Scripture Verses:
Acts 8:9-24; 17:16-29; 1 Corinthians 12:1-3; Revelation 12:7-9

Friends plead: "Just try sniffing this; you'll forget all the problems you're having in math."

Television preaches: "The more money you have, the happier you are."

Parents fume: "If you don't start working on your grades now, you'll never make it into a good college; you'll be a nobody!"

Good and evil aren't always black and white. Evil is often disguised as good, and it's sometimes hard for preteens to stand for the truth.

This lesson helps young people explore the nature of evil and discover how to recognize its influences in their lives.

Opening

Paper Clip Challenge

(For this activity, you'll need paper clips and a black marker.)

Before the session, bend a paper clip into an unusual form. Then subtly mark one end with a black marker. Form a circle, and give each person a paper clip. Show your bent paper clip to kids at close range, but hide the mark you made on it.

Say: **I'm going to give my paper clip to the person next to me. That person should quickly bend his or her paper clip to look just like mine, without letting anyone else see which is the original and which is the copy. Then that person should turn to the next person in the circle and ask him or her to choose the original. After that person chooses between the two, he or she should bend his or her paper clip to look just like the one chosen, then ask the next person to choose the original. We'll continue around the circle until it's my turn.**

When it's your turn, find your original paper clip. More than likely, someone at some point will have picked a copy. Show kids the mark you made on the paper clip. Ask:

● How hard was it to tell the difference between the original and the copy?

● What's the only sure way you could find which paper clip was the original?

Say: **Sometimes it's hard to know what's real and what's an imitation. God is real, but Satan has made many cheap, hollow imitations. The only way to tell the original from the fake is to ask the creator—God.**

Reflection and Application

PØWER PLAY

(For this activity, you'll need magazines, newspapers, scissors, a steel trash can, paper, pens, and matches.)

Hand out magazines, newspapers, and scissors to students. Ask kids to cut out pictures or headlines that represent power to them, such as money, health clubs, weapons, politicians, business people, and universities. As kids look for pictures and headlines, place a match on a table in front of them.

After five minutes or so, gather the clippings, and place them on the table in front of kids. Form three groups, and pass out a sheet of paper and a pen to each group.

Say: **Each group should rank the items on this table from most powerful to least powerful. On your paper, write the most powerful item at the top, and work your way down the paper to the least powerful item.**

Allow kids to look at the items, and encourage group discussion. After about five minutes, ask each group to tell about its ranking. Compare the three lists, and ask the entire group to vote on a most powerful and least powerful item. If kids choose the match as the most powerful item, congratulate them.

Otherwise, say: **Your lists are all well thought out. But the most powerful item on the table is this match.**

Pick up the match. Say: **Let me demonstrate.**

Take kids outside. Dump all the clippings into a steel trash can. Light the match, and set fire to the clippings. Or light just a corner of one clipping to illustrate the point. Ask:

● **How did you feel when I showed you the power of the match? Why?**

● **How is this match like God's power?**

Say: **The clippings are just pictures of the real thing. They have no real power. But the match is the real thing. It has power. Satan tries to fool us in the same way. He shows us pictures of things** we think are powerful—like the magical powers in horror movies or on television—and convinces us these are more powerful than what God has to offer. But Satan is a liar. And God is holding a match.

The Bible Experience

EXPØSING FRAUDS

(For this activity, you'll need Bibles, chalkboard or newsprint, chalk or marker, paper, and pens.)

Say: **It's sometimes easy to be deceived into believing something is true when it's really false. And we aren't the only ones who've been taken in by deception. Early Christians had the same trouble. Even though many had seen Jesus in person and had witnessed his power and heard the truth of his words, they were still tempted to believe in Satan's false gods.**

Form groups of no more than four. Assign each group one of the following Scripture passages: Acts 8:9-24; Acts 17:16-29; and Revelation 12:7-9. Have groups read their passages. While they're reading, write the following discussion questions on a chalkboard or newsprint:

For Acts 8:9-24:
● Why was Simon fascinated with the healings he saw?
● What was Simon's motive in asking the disciples for their power?
● Why did Peter criticize Simon?

For Acts 17:16-29:
● Do you think it's easier to worship a material object—such as an idol—than it is to worship a God you can't see with your eyes? Why or why not?
● Why was Paul so confident God is real and living?

For Revelation 12:7-9:
● Why do you think Satan tried to take over heaven?
● Why did God's angels throw Satan to earth?
● What do you think Satan's attitude toward God's children—you and me—is?

Have students write their answers on paper, then talk about their answers within their groups. Have groups report their discoveries.

IDOL SEARCH

(For this activity, you'll need a pen and a copy of the "Idol Search" handout [p. 105] for each person.)

Say: **In 1 Corinthians 12:1-3, Paul says the people followed "mute idols" before they followed Jesus. Idols were statues made of stone or wood that people put their faith and trust in. People looked to these dead objects for comfort, guidance, and power.**

Give each person an "Idol Search" handout (p. 105) and a pen. Have kids complete the handout.

Gather students, and ask them to explain why they circled certain objects on the handout. Then have students each choose one thing they circled that they've been tempted to idolize. Have them turn over their handouts and write a commitment to God to turn away from that idol.

Form a circle. One by one, have kids place their papers in the center of the circle. As they return to the circle, have them face outward. Then say: **When we turn away from idols, we need to turn toward God, and he will shower us with his love.**

Go around the circle, saying one thing you're thankful for about each student. As you thank kids, turn them back around to face inward. Have kids put their arms around each other for a group hug.

Closing

TRASH YOUR IDOLS

(For this activity, you'll need the "Idol Search" handouts from the previous activity and a trash can.)

Have students make paper airplanes out of their "Idol Search" handouts. Line students against a wall, and place a trash can ten to twenty feet away from them. One by one, have kids fly their airplanes into the trash can. Allow kids to get as close as necessary to fly them into the trash can. Then have kids repeat after you: **God, I'll throw these idols away so I can follow you only.**

IDOL SEARCH

Circle the objects in the picture that could be worshipped as idols.

Permission to photocopy this handout from *More Smart Choices for Preteen Kids* granted for local church use.
Copyright © Group Publishing, Inc., P.O. Box 481, Loveland, CO 80539.

Goal:

To help preteens avoid materialism and follow Jesus.

Scripture Verses:

Luke 1:46-55; John 13:5-17

Living in a Material World

We live in a world in which success is measured by how much money we make and how many "toys" we own. As a result, people are often motivated by a desire to "have it all." God, however, measures success in a different way. He wants us to use our gifts to serve him and others. That's the example Christ gave throughout his earthly life.

This lesson teaches preteens what it means to truly follow Jesus, even though they live in a materialistic world.

Opening

SEARCH FOR SUCCESS

(For this activity, you'll need magazines, newspapers, newsprint, tape, and markers.)

Collect magazine and newspaper pictures of famous people such as sports stars, movie stars, and politicians. Tape pictures on sheets of newsprint, leaving lots of space under each picture. Hang the newsprint around the room. Also hang a blank sheet marked "OTHER" so students can nominate people you missed.

Give each person a marker, and then instruct kids to walk around the room and vote for the three most successful people by signing their own names under the pictures of the famous people. When they've finished, declare the stars with the most signatures "the most successful people in the world."

Then ask:

● **Why did you rate these people as the most successful?**

Then say: **Today we're going to examine success. From your answers, we've already heard some messages about what it means to be successful. However, I want us to look at how God defines success. We may be surprised by what we find out!**

winninc in a MaTeRial WORLD

(For this activity, you'll need card games and enough copies of the "Winning in a Material World" handout [p. 111] for each person to receive a role sheet.)

Form groups of six or fewer. Give each group a card game such as Go Fish, Crazy Eights, or War.

Before kids start playing, ask one person from each group to serve as an observer. Take the observers aside, and inform them it's their responsibility to watch each person in the group during the game. Show them the "Winning in a Material World" role sheets (p. 111) so they know what to watch for. Have them take notes on how the players act and what their actions do to the game, but don't have observers say anything to the group.

Next, hand out the "Living in a Material World" role sheets (p. 111) to the other group participants, and tell them not to let anyone see what their roles are in the game. Don't tell kids they all have the same role. Instruct the players to remember it's important to stay in their roles at all times while playing the game.

Let the games go on for five to eight minutes. Watch for any deteriorating relationships. Then ask observers to report what happened in each of their groups and who did what to whom.

After the reports, ask:

● **How did you feel as you were playing the game?**
● **How did you feel toward the other players?**
● **How is being successful in the world sometimes like this?**
● **How does this method of achieving success affect people?**

Say: **You've just experienced what it means to live in a materialistic world. It's a part of our nature called sin. Our natural desire is to get ahead and be successful—no matter what it costs. The messages to be the best and have the most are not only all around us, but they're also in us—and we all struggle with them at times.**

Let's check out the areas we have problems in. Finish this sentence: "The area in which I always want to be number one is..."

Have several students share how they'd complete the sentence. You might give a few examples to get them started thinking, such as "at school," "with brothers and sisters," or "in sports." Then say: **Jesus wants us to look at this world and the people in it in a whole new way. We're going to examine a few Scripture passages that will help us see success in a very different way.**

SONGS OF SUCCESS

(For this activity, you'll need Bibles, newsprint, and markers.)

Say: **One way the world communicates its values is through music.** Ask:

● **What popular songs have you heard that are about success or material things?**

● **What attitudes toward success and material things do most of those songs promote?**

After kids respond, form groups of four or five. Give each group a Bible, a sheet of newsprint, and a marker. Instruct the groups to divide their newsprint into two columns. Tell kids to draw symbols in the first column that show popular music's definition of success.

When they've finished, say: **Mary, the mother of Jesus, sang or spoke a song about success shortly before Jesus was born. However, her idea of success is a little different from the music we've just talked about.**

Have the groups read Luke 1:46-55 aloud together. After reading the passage, have groups each draw symbols in the second column that show Mary's definition of success.

After they've finished drawing their pictures, have each group appoint a representative to explain the symbols they chose for the two sides of the newsprint. After the explanations, ask:

● **How do these symbols reflect the two views of success?**

● **Who (or what) gets left out of the picture in popular music's view of success?**

● **What made Mary, the mother of Jesus, happy?**

● **What appealing and not-so-appealing things does Mary's success include?**

Give each group another sheet of newsprint. Tell kids to read John 13:5-17 and draw symbols representing Jesus' idea of success.

When they've finished, have groups share their symbols. Then ask:

● **How do you think the disciples felt when Jesus washed their feet?**

● **On what levels does Jesus put servants and masters?**

● **How would you have reacted if you'd been there when Jesus was washing feet?**

Make a Commitment

A WASH

(For this activity, you'll need a damp washcloth for each person.)

Gather kids in one large group, and give them each a damp washcloth. Tell students to sit in a circle facing outward, next to someone they trust, and to place their washcloths on the floor in front of them. Darken the room as much as possible.

Say: **Jesus wants us to care about each other so much that we're willing to do even unpleasant tasks for each other. Because of the way we're dressed today, it would be hard to wash each other's feet. But let's try to get a feel for what Jesus was talking about.**

Ask kids to sit in silence, with their eyes closed, and think about their own struggles for success. You may need to occasionally remind the group to remain silent.

After a few minutes, say:

● **If you've ever found yourself wanting to be number one, open your eyes.**

● **If you've ever talked negatively about someone, look at your washcloth.**

● **If you've ever been jealous of a friend who has gotten something you haven't, pick up your washcloth.**

● **If you've ever cheated, use the washcloth to wash your left hand.**

● **If you've been embarrassed to be seen with someone, use the washcloth to wash your right hand.**

Now have kids form pairs by turning to the person on the left. Say:

● **If you think this person can be successful in God's eyes, wash his or her left hand.**

● **If you think this person can be a successful servant, wash his or her right hand.**

● **If you think this person continues to grow in learning to follow Christ, give him or her your washcloth.**

Closing

AUTOGRAPH HOUNDS

(For this activity, you'll need paper and pens.)

Give each student a sheet of paper and a pen; then have everyone stand. Say: **This is a special autograph page. You usually get the autographs of people who are successful or famous. This is your chance to get the autographs of people who, like you, can achieve** fame in God's eyes every day. They are successful servants, people following Jesus' example. Go to other kids in the class, and have them sign your paper while you sign theirs. As you give your autograph, give words of encouragement related to serving God. For example, you might say, "You can serve God because you're so caring" or "Your creativity helps you serve God well."

Encourage kids to collect the autographs of other successful servants at your church, such as a favorite Sunday school teacher, the usher who always says hello, or their youth group leaders.

Finish by praying that God will help each person be a successful servant.

winning in a Material World

- -

Role Sheet

You need to win this game. For you there are no rules other than you must win. You can cheat, lie, or do anything else in your power to win. That's all that's important. Don't let anyone else know what your role is.

- -

Role Sheet

You need to win this game. For you there are no rules other than you must win. You can cheat, lie, or do anything else in your power to win. That's all that's important. Don't let anyone else know what your role is.

- -

Role Sheet

You need to win this game. For you there are no rules other than you must win. You can cheat, lie, or do anything else in your power to win. That's all that's important. Don't let anyone else know what your role is.

- -

Permission to photocopy this handout from *More Smart Choices for Preteen Kids* granted for local church use.
Copyright © Group Publishing, Inc., P.O. Box 481, Loveland, CO 80539.

SCRIPTURE INDEX